THE
ALCHEMY
WITHIN

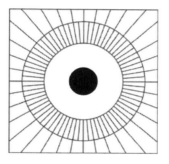

180 DAYS TO RELEASE &
TRANSCEND SELF-DOUBT

JAMIE VARON

For any distribution inquiries, please visit jamievaron.com

FIRST EDITION

Designed by Jamie Varon

ISBN: 979-8-218-43294-2

When you're looking outside of yourself for the answers, just remember: *the alchemy begins within*

INTRODUCTION

What I know is that everything changes *outside* of you when everything changes *within* you.

Self-doubt is only the symptom of the root cause—you do not trust yourself, trust the process, or believe in your resiliency.

Too often, we put the onus on achievements and big goals and a host of situations outside of our control, waiting for it all to line up, to finally get to that sacred destination where it all clicks into place, where self-doubt is no longer an issue. We think the answer is outside of ourselves. We think the next big achievement is going to save us, prove that we are worthy of our existence.

We think our fulfillment is in fulfilling a list of goals.

But how many times have you met a goal and been disappointed at your reaction to it? *That's it?*

You start to realize that actually the *pursuit* of the goal—the process, progress, and practice where you spend the majority of your time—was actually the most fulfilling part. You want to get back into the pursuit so you can get the high of diligence, dedication, devotion. You become obsessed with the space before the results. The fulfillment, therefore, is *within*. Your purpose is how you *do* your life. How you *exist* in your life. Your peace is gained by knowing that.

Whatever happens outside of you is, by nature, outside of your control. What is within your locus of control is how you interact with yourself from the inside out. The relationship you maintain with your inner self.

Self-doubt cannot coexist with self-belief, self-trust, and self-love. When you have those internally, that will powerfully determine your quality of life.

The answers you're looking for are within.

The alchemy desired to transcend self-doubt—it's within.

It *all* starts within.

I hope you have the courage to recognize this and go on the greatest journey of your life. The journey to know yourself and to live by your authenticity, to call in what's uniquely meant for you.

Your true self is calling. It's time to answer. Begin at Day 1.

Love,
Jamie Varon

DAY 1

I know it can be hard to believe that anything can change, but if you start doing things a little differently right now, they will. They *have* to. Even devoting thirty minutes per day to yourself will significantly impact how confident you feel. Just honoring one thing you want to change, and committing to it, can expand a whole world of possibility within you. We underestimate the power of small steps and overestimate big, drastic changes. Maybe you don't need to leave, move, quit, set your whole life on fire. Maybe you need to just readjust, tweak, shift, honor, accept. Or, maybe this is the year for you to burn it down. Trust you'll know when you need to know. Just please don't give into despair and apathy. Not with yourself. There is always change and renewal awaiting you. You can alchemize an entirely new life within you starting today. Today can be your fresh start if you decide that it is.

DAY 2

How about you don't have to build an empire? Or dominate an industry? Or be the number one at anything? What if you simply built a lovely life that makes you feel happy, that brings you joy, that is generative and supportive? What if you healed the parts of you that need more and more and more? What if you redefined what success looks and feels like to you? What if you decided enough is enough? What if you felt satisfied in the right here, the right now? What if you realized your life is likely a lot closer to your ideal than you ever thought? What if changing the filter in which you view your life makes everything that much more vibrant? How much open empty space would be left for your joy if you stopped thinking you needed to earn it? How much time could you spend in the actual living of your life if you let go of striving for more? How much more beautiful would *this* moment, right here, become for you?

DAY 3

When you start demanding a better life, be aware that before it shows up, you'll have to go through an extensive inventory of all the reasons you believe you don't deserve it, can't have it, won't ever get it. That's why when you start loving yourself, you need to confront all the ways in which you have betrayed yourself first. There is no newness that can spring forth without the desolation and clearing out. There is no space without letting go. There is no "better" unless you examine why you think you don't get to have it. This is an essential part of the process. It's why staying the same is so much easier. Staying the same isn't confronting. It doesn't ask questions. It's not demanding. It doesn't require awareness or examination. All it requires is that you stay still and comfortable and never ask for anything at all.

DAY 4

You will get it all right only to watch parts of it fall apart again. You will get "off track" only to realize there is no damn track. There is only your life and how you approach it each day. You will stumble and forget lessons you thought were ingrained. You will heal only to see it unravel. You will have effortless days and then you will have effortful days. You will progress and then take five steps back and then move forward in a totally different way that you'll realize was necessary, but all of this will only make sense with the benefit of retrospect. You will be consistently humbled by how much there is still to discover about yourself and the world. Your life will be a series of chapters and books. It will not look like anyone else's. It will be hard and it will be magical and you will never know which one is around the corner. You will get lost and found over and over again. None of this is an indication that you are doing life "wrong." In fact, it's an indication you are doing it very "right." Because you are alive to it all. How incredible, to be in a perpetual state of becoming, growth, and evolvement.

DAY 5

Your life belongs to you. It's not selfish to want your life to benefit you. It's not selfish to ask: What am I getting out of this? And if the answer is "not much," it's not selfish to walk away. It's amazing to be humble and empathic and understanding, but you are not a martyr. You are allowed to be first on your priority list. Your life is something you *create*, not something you have to *endure*. Yes, you have to work hard to create the life you want, but it's better than living on autopilot, letting other people decide what your direction will be. I hope you step up to your life. That you realize that it's not selfish to want the best for yourself. It's not selfish to create a life that makes you happy, that isn't waiting for validation from others. It's never selfish to build a loving, beautiful home within yourself.

DAY 6

The ego boasts. The soul shares. The ego isolates. The soul includes. The ego creates pressure. The soul creates change. The ego tells you that you will never be happy unless you get this and this and this and this. The soul says you can be happy right now. The ego tells you that you'll never be enough so keep striving. The soul asks what's enough and why do you care. The ego divides. The soul unifies. The ego is that sinking pit in the middle of your stomach, shame and guilt. The soul is that feeling of peace you get in the middle of a Tuesday when the sun is shining and nothing is perfect but somehow everything is. The ego keeps you searching outside of you, insatiable and relentless for more. The soul says what you have inside of you is the whole Universe so what's *out there* that isn't within? The ego provides a never ending list of reasons you are unhappy. The soul provides a never ending list of reasons to be content, right now, right here. Which part of you do you listen to most? The punishing litany of dissatisfaction from the ego or the soul alchemy available within?

DAY 7

Be in the day you're in. In the season you're in. In the feeling you're in. You try so hard to escape to the past, to the future, to try to plan it all out, to brace yourself for uncertainty. You try to perfect the future in order to avoid the present. It'll get better later. One day, you'll be happy. One day, when you get it all right and perfect and check off the list, you'll finally have space for your joy. But what about the day you're in? The moment you have right now? Where have you gone? Don't you want to be there, too? What if you're missing the lesson, the signs, the magic of right here? Nothing in the future gives you permission to bask in joy. Nothing slows down until *you* slow it down. If you can't be in today, what makes you think you'll be fully present to tomorrow? Be in the day you're in. What is happening for you here? Where are you being led? What is your heart saying? Don't prolong it. Be in this day. Let that be enough. Your joy is here. Your life is here. The future is always coming but you never get this moment—this exact one—ever again. Don't miss being alive to your days while you're lucky enough to have them.

DAY 8

Have the audacity to love yourself even though you're not perfect. So, you haven't done all the things you want to do yet. You've failed at times. You've made mistakes. You've hurt people. You've been hurt. Sometimes you look in the mirror and you wish to see someone different. Sometimes you don't do all the things you need to do. Sometimes you avoid what is best for you. Sometimes you get anxious and see no way out from it all. But sometimes you smile and your entire world gets more vibrant. Sometimes a walk in the sunshine feels like magic. Sometimes you look in the mirror and see a person you love. Maybe those failures have led you to what is most meant for you. Have you ever trusted in your timing so beautifully you feel remarkable peace? Have the audacity to love an imperfect person. Have the audacity to believe you are worthy of love even when you don't have it all figured out or lined up or smooth or flat. Have this really wild idea that you deserve love *no matter what.*

DAY 9

I don't care how successful you are. How much money you have. What your body looks like. I want to know how you spend your time. If you know how to be happy, how to heal yourself from the pain of your past, how to sit with uncomfortable feelings, how to connect with people in a way that isn't just surface-level conversation. Do you know how to rest? Do you know how to be kind to yourself and, in extension, kind to others? Are you extracting the most from this life? I hope you know how to be content, how to know when enough is enough. I hope you can sit still, be alone, love your own company as much as the company of others. I hope the way you speak to yourself is loving. I hope the people who you surround yourself with know you, the *real you*. I hope you are courageous enough to be exactly who you are. I hope you are brave more than you are checking off societal signposts. I hope you don't wake up too late and wish you'd done it all differently. I hope you have enough open space to know yourself, to know what you want, and to pursue that with patience and resiliency. I hope you are doing this life *for you*, truly and honestly and openly.

DAY 10

Please set standards for the people you want in your life. It's not selfish. It's not rude. It's imperative. You are allowed to determine who gets access to you. You are allowed to want people in your life who make you feel light and supported. You can set that standard. It's *your* life. Don't forget that.

DAY 11

In a world obsessed with instant gratification and quick fixes, putting in the daily work and consistency to build a life of true happiness can often feel isolating. Making changes that benefit your well-being comes with grief, too. People lost. Experiences that don't fit anymore. A life that is a little less certain than it was when you were going along with the tide of others. Making good decisions for yourself might not look the way society thinks they should. When you make decisions outside the beaten path, it's empowering and freeing and it can also be difficult, sad, lonely. But, nurturing your long-term self instead of your insatiable short-term self puts you at an advantage. It makes you happier. It makes you clearer. It gives you so much. If you're in that space today of choosing the more difficult route over the conventional one, I hope you know how brave you are. It's not easy to go against the grain, but it's fulfilling. Stay the course. The discomfort is a sign of growth.

DAY 12

They tell us: Don't "settle." Never settle. Keep grinding. Never give up. If you're settling, you're failing. But, we became so obsessed with never settling that we forgot to *get settled*. To calm down. To know when it's time to be content and satisfied. And that doesn't mean you won't want more or that you won't grow or that you won't challenge yourself ever again. But it's okay to just... live in your life. To know you are not a perpetual problem in need of fixing. To enjoy your blessings. To look around at what you've built and feel... satisfied. It may not be perfect. It may not be exactly what you thought it would be. But it's *yours*. And that means a lot more than you think. It's got your signature all over it. Enjoying that isn't settling. It's letting yourself settle in.

DAY 13

I don't care if you live your "best" life. I hope you live your freest life. Your most unburdened life. Your lightest life. I hope your life is a patchwork of lessons and trials and joys and mistakes and growth and evolution and expansion. I hope you understand that rejection, failure, disappointment means you care, you're trying, you're out there in life, alive to it. I hope your life feels beautiful to you more than it looks beautiful to everyone else. I hope you're free. And that you keep freeing yourself. From who you thought you should be. From who society told you to be. From heavy expectations and weighty ambition. I hope you know when you're in a moment you'll remember forever. I hope you know how good you have it when it's good. And I hope your life is an ongoing evolution, a constant becoming. I hope you shrug off old selves with ease. I hope you leave empty space in your life for the unknown, the magic, the surprises, the unexpected. I hope you don't just aim for "best" and instead aim for full, whole, ever-evolving, unconfined, and unrestrained. Mostly, I hope you take the path that is *meant for you*, not the one expected of you.

DAY 14

Success is waking up every morning and *liking yourself*. Isn't it? Isn't that the only real goal? Which means you have to show up and write in your little journal and take your little walks and exclaim at the beauty of trees and take note of when the flowers bloom and when the leaves fall and when it's watermelon season. Because you can't like yourself if you also neglect yourself. And you can't be alive if you don't notice your life while you have it. And it means that if there's something on your soul that you feel you need to create, you need to water it, carve out a bit of time in your day to make sure you give your gifts enough space to grow. It means you need people in your life who see the real you, and support that. It means you can't be the biggest barrier in your way. It means you need to do the inner work to clear out the immense clutter of limiting beliefs so that you may be free to meet the truest version of yourself. It means you focus on being present with yourself so that every day, you wake up knowing you are loved. Now, *that* is success.

DAY 15

If you feel "off track" please remember there is no "track." This is your life. It ebbs and flows and twists and halts and speeds up. *It all belongs.* Stop trying to be a robot who is productive and perfect all the time. You're not a robot. You're a human. Be alive to it all.

DAY 16

This has to be the time when you become your own best friend. I hope this is the time you commit to being your own ally. To learning the depth of your resilience. To saying kinder things to yourself. To being the one who cheers you on. Life will get *lighter* when you have your own back. And I hope, if you commit to nothing else, that you commit to yourself. That you learn to love the parts of yourself that have been hard to love. That you are a compassionate voice within. That you hear yourself over the noise of the world. That you know you can handle pretty much anything because you have you this time. Commit to that. Make that a priority. The relationship you have with yourself is forever. Be your own fiercest champion. Learn to accept what you have been taught to not love. Be a soft place to land in a harsh world. It's worth it. You're worth it. Your own love is worth fighting for.

DAY 17

The big things are only amplified when you romanticize the small things. If you think you need more in your life in order to feel grateful, you will never have enough. If you think the small things are worth ignoring, the big moments will be a letdown. If you sacrifice constantly in one area in order to get fulfillment in a different area, you'll end up wishing you hadn't lost so much on the way up to whatever summit you think you'll arrive at. You'll miss what you sacrificed. Your fulfillment is a continuously evolving space within you. It can be found in the bloom of spring flowers, in the desolation of winter, in the middle of your biggest dream coming true. The trick is in recognizing that it's not about *one* thing. It's about *everything*. Fulfillment is presence. Being alive to your life while you have it. Noticing the beauty all around you. Getting out there, living, and knowing what it is to be a soul having a human experience.

DAY 18

Everything starts with loving yourself. Love yourself enough to take your dreams seriously. Love yourself enough to make mistakes and keep going. Love yourself enough that you know you matter, that your voice matters, that you are worthy of what you most want. Love yourself enough that you are your own fiercest advocate. Love yourself so much that nobody in this world can define you. Love yourself so well, others have to rise to your level. Love yourself so others have a standard they have to meet. Love yourself so much that you become an open, fertile space for what's meant for you to *come right in.*

DAY 19

Self-care is recognizing that what you want to do and what is best for you are not always the same thing.

Self-love is acting on behalf of what is best for you, even if it doesn't temporarily satisfy you.

Boundaries are how you allot the time and energy it takes to do the above.

DAY 20

You don't need anyone's permission. You are not meant to be small and palatable. To take everything lying down. To make life easier for everyone else as your life becomes harder. You are not here to birth the dreams of others. To make constant sacrifices for the betterment of others. To keep chipping away bite-sized pieces to give to others. To talk in hushed words, never letting truth spill from your lips. It is not selfish to be directly involved in your own life. It is not selfish to keep something for yourself, to want, to not give away everything in order to make others happier. It is not selfish to want happiness, joy, inspiration, desire—for yourself. You are allowed to be hungry. You are allowed to feast, too.

DAY 21

Self-care, rituals, habits, morning routines, all of these things are meant to *soften* you toward your own life. To bring you closer to yourself. To make you feel good and safe on a consistent basis. They aren't checkmarks on a To Do list, steeped in shame and causing more and more stress. They are your healing, your unlearning, your freedom, your trust in yourself. The act of keeping your own promises to yourself is the point. Feeling good is the point.

DAY 22

This is permission to have specifics about the way you want your life to be. Give yourself permission to build it, even if it takes longer than you think it should take. Give yourself space to step away from your default and assess whether it's serving you. You are worthy of the life you envision. Maybe it won't go exactly the way you think it will. But it's the act of wanting, of believing in your own desires, in knowing that you deserve that which you can imagine—*that* is the essential part. You are allowed to want more from this one life you get.

DAY 23

I promise you: it's never too late to be who you truly are. Maybe you wish you'd started earlier and you're worried your time has passed. But, it's never too late to course-correct. It's never too late to pick up a passion that makes you feel alive. It's never too late to be honest with yourself, to carve out space in your life for what feels right. Would it have been easier if you had started ten years ago? Maybe. But maybe consider that your timing isn't supposed to be like any one else's. This is *your* life. Maybe you're exactly where you're meant to be. It's never too late to turn around and rediscover parts of yourself you've left behind. Use your regret as fuel. Use your regret as a path forward. You didn't begin yesterday or last year or a decade before but you know what? You can begin today. And that means everything. You are not behind. It's never too late. Don't keep looking back. Start looking forward. Do now what you wish you had done before. It's your time.

DAY 24

Before self-love becomes a liberation, it is first a burden. Well, there's the anger at who treated you poorly when you didn't know to ask for better treatment. The anger at yourself for what you've allowed. There's the grief for lost time. There's the strangling necessity to push people, things, ideas out, out, *out* because there's no room for them. There's the loneliness and isolation that accompanies the growth of self. There's the new boundary lines, the new range of the word no, the opening of eyes that would rather be shut, and the terrifying realization that love isn't synonymous with joy. It's synonymous with growth.

DAY 25

Something beautiful happens when you stop waiting to be chosen and instead choose yourself. When you love yourself first. When you can be alone with the shape of yourself. When you stop running away from your truth. The right people start to show up. The right opportunities suddenly align. All the hustling you were doing, trying to make yourself more worthy, stops feeling right, and instead you get into the flow of life. And everything you thought you'd have to earn and strive for seems to come a lot more easily. When you choose you, everything and everyone has to rise to that level. And all the good things you thought you'd have to force arrive in perfect timing. Yes, you need to show up. Yes, you need to work. But, it'll be with the right people, the right opportunities, and the kind of life that lights you up from the inside. Because *you* are lit up from the inside.

DAY 26

Being kind and loving to yourself will not lead to complacency. Love works better. If you do everything from a place of loving yourself, life becomes so much easier, lighter, fun. Be your own greatest ally. Support yourself. Be compassionate toward you. This will lead you to beautiful, generative places. It will lead you to what is meant for you. It will lead you to the people, opportunities, and situations that will confirm the love you feel within. Your own love is a safe space. You are allowed to be your own best friend. Encouraging yourself will work better. You do not need to be your own worst enemy in order to do more, and become more. When you love yourself, your whole life arranges and aligns to magic. You do more of what brings you joy. What doesn't serve you naturally falls away. Let yourself change and grow. Let yourself be loved. Let your own love be the standard in your life. You don't have to earn it. You just have to recognize that power you already have *within*.

DAY 27

You have changed. You have grown. You have healed. Even when it feels like nothing has progressed the way you expected it to, you know that you are reacting differently. You look at yourself differently. You act differently. Something has shifted. Maybe many something's have shifted. It might seem uncertain right now. Maybe you feel a little lost, a little unmoored, a little unsettled. That is because you are stretching into a new version of yourself. You're going somewhere you haven't gone yet. That is your path. That is where you are headed. Trust in that. Trust that you have come so far. You may not have a sense of what's next, but you know yourself better now. You have gone to the depths of yourself. You've got you this time. Don't worry too much. Let yourself flow. Let yourself gently become the next iteration of yourself. Be proud of you. This hasn't been easy, but now you know the strength of your resilience, the depths of your courage. And that is worth everything.

DAY 28

You might spend so much time planning for your life that you don't actually live it. You might spend so much time healing, you forget that you have to take your healed self out into the world eventually. The point is not to perfect living before you have a life. The point is to make mistakes, experiment, fail, get rejected, disappointed, and report back to yourself what you've learned. The point isn't to retreat from the unknown, because out there in the world might inspire an emotion, might get you out of your comfort zone, might make you uncomfortable. You know, you can be uncomfortable. You'll survive. You are more resilient than you think. You don't need to let fear run your life. Get out there, make some mistakes, learn, grow, evolve. That is the point. That is what makes a life. The point is not to find one spot to stay in forever, because if you're not growing, you're not living.

DAY 29

Maybe you got it wrong. Maybe instead of trying to make it all bigger you should have made it smaller and simpler. Maybe instead of trying to be the best you should just try. Maybe it's the ordinary that's truly extraordinary. Maybe it's the will to like how it is just as it is that saves you and spares you. Maybe instead of going for the end, working and working for the reward, you should have made it all so fun and engaging and wonderful that you forgot why you started in the first place, because oh, isn't it beautiful there? Where you ended up? It isn't where you thought you'd be, but maybe you should have been going there all along.

JAMIE VARON

DAY 30

Maybe you've got more to learn, more to heal, more to unlearn, more to accept. But take a moment to remember that you have grown significantly. There are places within you that no longer ache. There are triggers that you no longer trip over. There are situations that no longer plague you, memories that no longer gut you, and people that you never even think about anymore. You have come so far. It's easy to lose sight of that when your eyes are already on the next thing. But sink in here for a moment. Remember where you were and where you are now. You trust yourself a little more, maybe. You hold yourself a little closer, perhaps. There are storms within you that used to rattle everything, but are now quieter. There are emotions you are no longer afraid of expressing, words you can say clearly, stories you can tell without shaking. You have grown. You have taken steps forward. You know you have. Now you need to acknowledge it, too. Sink in here. Be proud of yourself.

DAY 31

Quitting is powerful.

Leaving is powerful.

"No" is powerful.

It's an energetic way of saying: *I deserve better.*
And it creates an automatic opening for better
to come right in.

DAY 32

When you understand that resistance and doubt are a completely natural and normal part of being human, those states of being will not shake your foundation that much. Yes, they will be uncomfortable. But if you keep showing up regardless, *that* becomes your superpower to never let fear, doubt, or resistance define you. Even if you show up and nothing happens, it's the sacred act of making space that allows for flow. Consistency does not mean every single day. It's about intentional time. Carving out the moment. Resistance and fear cannot stop you if you're unwilling to be deterred. The more you allow resistance to steal time from you, the more it will. It's such a tidy excuse to avoid the messy work of forward movement. Be unshakable instead.

DAY 33

Don't give up on yourself. Ever. Believe in change. Believe in fresh starts. Believe that an hour, a month, a year can change anything and everything. Believe in a transformation. A breakthrough. A breakdown leading to a breakthrough. Keep healing and growing, not so you can be a "better" version of yourself, but so you can be a *freer* version of yourself. Free yourself from limits, and limiting beliefs, and limited personal narratives. Believe that you can change your story, see your past through a new filter, let go, and find yourself in a future full of magic and synchronicities and right places, right time. Let go of plans, control, grasping, clenching. Sometimes you have to let life lead you. Sometimes you have to take a deep inhale, a big exhale, and admit to yourself that you still have hope. Don't let the world harden you, try as it will to do so. Believe in you. Start within. Free yourself. Listen to yourself. Honor yourself. Let that still voice within be the guiding light for a while. Exhale.

DAY 34

"If I let myself be satisfied, I'll end up doing less." Yes. That's the whole point. Less of what you think you should be doing to prove yourself worthy. And more of what you want to be doing. Most of us have schedules maximized to the last hour, without knowing why we keep saying yes, why we're committing to so much. We spend time with people we don't like, afraid to say no. We take on another responsibility, thinking that frenetic activity is what it looks like to be successful. And we keep our contentment on an unreachable horizon. Be more productive. That'll solve it. Always hustling. No days off. No rest. You'll sleep when you're dead, apparently. Becoming radically satisfied is the antidote. You'll do less. And that will be okay. Less of what you're doing to prove and more of what you actually want to do. Less obligation, more lit up hell yes's. Less feeling like your time is something to fill with other people's demands and more of your time is something to fill with your joy. So yes, you'll do less. But you'll gain so much *more*.

DAY 35

Nobody is going to finally give you permission to love your life, your body, your existence on this Earth. You do that for *you*. You don't need permission to enjoy the sunshine on your face, the feel of warm water on your skin, the laugh you make when something catches you off guard. Stop hoarding your joy. You deserve it all now. Act accordingly.

DAY 36

It's hard to stay hopeful when it feels like your moment has passed. When everyone else seems to have it figured out. When you're buried under the weight of *it's too late* and *I should have started earlier*. But, there is still time. You are allowed to take it at your pace. You can't control the timeline of your life, but you can control whether you allow yourself to be discouraged. Resist the urge to be "realistic." You don't have to light your life on fire, but there is always space to keep going. Be patient. Often, when you feel the strongest urge to give up is the moment to go deeper. Release your expectations of how it should have gone and let it go as it's going. This whole experience, this strength you're building, this trust in yourself—it's all part of it. It's wisdom. Later, it becomes the story of your life: when you were brave and bold and wanted to give up, but never did.

DAY 37

You are never behind on your own life. It all arrives in perfect timing if you don't give up on yourself. You haven't even accessed the full breadth of the genius and gifts that live within you. The worst thing you can do is assume there's a time limit on your dreams. There isn't. There is always a chance to start anew. There is always inspiration to be found. There is always a will with a dream. Don't let this narrow-minded world and society try to tell you there's a cut-off to your own brilliance. There really isn't.

DAY 38

Disappointment can be information. Maybe it didn't happen for you when you expected it to happen for you, because you needed to learn something valuable. You needed to ignore timelines and ages and expiration dates and focus on the work in front of you. What brings you alive? Why do you do this? Why does it matter? You might need to learn how to give yourself time and space to do what you're capable of doing. To let go of how it must be and lean into how it is. To see possibility in small and unlikely places. To let your talent feed you, belong to you. To understand that life is long and you have time. To stop trying to be good for everyone else and instead be good for yourself. Are you having fun? Is it joyful? Do you like it? Instead of always asking am I good enough am I good enough am I good enough, maybe you need to see that's the wrong question to ask. Do you like it? Is this joyful to you? Are you being fed? Those are the answers that matter. That's the lesson of disappointment. Recalibration. Reflection. Back to you.

DAY 39

It's never too late to begin.

Start a business at 48.

Learn to play the guitar at 35.

Write your book at 62.

F*ck timelines.

Wherever you are, whoever you are, whatever your age, *your time is now.*

DAY 40

One day, maybe one day soon, the timing of your life will make sense. You'll understand that you were preparing for the next season of your life in ways that weren't clear in the moment. You'll recognize the magic at work, when you listen within, when you live by your own intuition and your own nudges and stop craving a road map given to you by someone else. You'll see just how expansive life becomes when you stop trying to fit yourself into smaller and smaller boxes, when you stop using age as a timeline, or external numbers as metrics of your value. When your value is intrinsic; when your worth is unconditional and from within you; when your soul is the thing being expressed—you can more readily see that you've been given exactly what you didn't know you needed in order to grow into the person you have become. It's when you shut off connection to yourself that you truly miss the magic of all the seasons of your life. It's when you use society as the map in which to tell you whether you're good at being good that there's no open space for what's meant for you. Be your own guide. Your own map. Your own magic.

DAY 41

You know, it could all work out for you. Maybe it's already finding a way to work out for you. But if you're so focused on it going a certain way, or doubtful that it'll work out, you might miss the way it's meant to unfold. Doubt blocks the magic. And maybe it's not going to work out the exact way you expect, but if you don't keep yourself open to new, better, different ways, then you miss the surprising, exciting unfolding. And it'll just find new ways to find you. It'll keep you blocked until you surrender and let go. It'll keep you circling the same lesson until you finally see what's trying to come forth for you. That's how life works. It's a series of clenching and letting go. Hopefulness with flexibility. Doing the work then letting the work speak for itself. Accepting what is and changing what you can't accept. Making a plan then staying open to a totally new plan. Life is a turning up and a turning down. Life wants your trust. When you give it, all you'll see are possibilities.

DAY 42

Do you want peace? Really? Because peace requires mental acuity that will get challenged every single day. Peace is not really peace if you have a set of conditions that need to be met in order for you to have it. "Protecting your peace" does not mean you exist in a bubble, far from anything or anyone that might trigger you. That's a pretend peace. That's a fragile peace. That's, frankly, not even peace. If you need to withdraw yourself from everyday life in order to be calm, that will make your life smaller. But if you can maintain a sense of tranquility no matter what is happening around you, responding calmly, and recognizing you have choice in your reactions to situations, that is true peace. That is choosing peace above all drama that wants to make you feel right or superior or justified. Choosing peace over everything means working on your mental patterns and reactions. It's not about isolating yourself and making your life extremely fragile. Knowing this is immense wisdom.

DAY 43

What's not meant for you will miss you. You have plans. You have ideas of what will make you happy. You construct it all in your mind. But what you really don't know is how it will feel once you're in it. So maybe that dream job you're feeling down about not getting was going to be a nightmare for you. Maybe that perfect person was only perfect on paper. Maybe that opportunity was only going to be a distraction from something else that's trying to come into your awareness. Maybe it's all working out for you beautifully, in ways you can't put into words, in perspectives that only become visible in retrospect. So, don't force it all to happen the way you think it should. Don't end up somewhere that was trying to miss you, simply because you were too intent on hustling your way into an ideal that might not even be good for you. Do your work. Take inspired actions. Be open to it unfolding better than expected. And allow what's meant to miss you skate right on by.

DAY 44

Maybe life isn't meant to be optimized to the very last second of your day. Maybe all these modern "conveniences" have done nothing but inconvenience your soul. Maybe while you're trying to squeeze more productivity and routine into your life, you are missing the fundamental point of what life is even about. What is the point of buying yourself more time if all you do with that time is use it to work? What are you working *toward*? Where does this road lead? One day you might optimize yourself right out of being a human. You may control every single emotion you've ever had. You may call that success. Be careful. Life is meant to be a little messy. A little uncontrolled. A little out of balance. Don't optimize so much you miss the essential part of being a human: the *being* part.

DAY 45

Trust that it's coming back. The inspiration. The answers. The vision. The energy. The joy. You can't be "on" all the time. You're not a machine. You're not a robot. There are so many valleys you must walk through in order to recognize the peaks. Your emotions are not just "good" or "bad." You're not just productive or not. You do not exist in that binary. You can't be defined that easily. You can't be summed up like that. Leave space for the dips. Let yourself appreciate the beauty of contrasts. Stop expecting yourself to never need a pause, a break, a lull. It's all part of it. Take an exhale. Let it all come to you when you least expect it. Go live. Go be. Go enjoy. Breathe and release. Let the next step find you with the sunshine on your face, lost in a moment.

DAY 46

The best decisions are the ones that people don't understand. When you make a decision from within, not everyone will get it. They will think you're doing something "wrong." But when you decide on something that feels right to you, even if it goes against conventional advice, you're living by your intuition. You are making authentic, potent decisions. Embrace being misunderstood. Too many people need validation for the decisions they make so their lives become predictable. They check off from a societal list of accomplishments. But when you listen to your inner wisdom, you don't use any list. You go where you are led. And that's a beautiful thing.

DAY 47

You are not a constant self-improvement project. It's okay to not always be out of your comfort zone. It's okay to let enough be enough for a while. It's okay to stop, and appreciate how far you've come. You have changed so much since this time last year. *Take notice.* Enjoy how much you've grown.

DAY 48

The world tries to tell us that you get to be happy about your life when others perceive it as successful. When you've won awards that other people give to you. When your work is received to acclaim that others give to you. When you can give off the perception of material wealth. Success is only success when others give you the title. But what about intrinsic success? If people perceive you as successful but you don't feel it within, what is the point? What is it worth? Believe it or not, you define worth for yourself. You either give your worth to others and tell them to decide for you. Or you decide your own worth. Either way, it belongs to you—as something you give away, or something you don't. The world tells you the measure of success is perception, how others view you. Yet, how you feel about your life is the only true measure of success. How you interpret your days. How you value yourself. How you perceive yourself. You can give the measuring stick to other people. Or you can take all the power back, throw out the damn stick, and focus on building a life that feels *so good*, you'll never feel compelled to outsource your worth again.

DAY 49

Your whole life will be a series of healing. That's how it works. You live, you uncover a layer, you are asked to go deeper, and you sink into a part of you that feels even more true than the person you were a year, a month, a week, a minute before. In many ways, it's about shedding. Shedding what holds you back from experiencing your life as it's happening. Shedding societal conditioning. Shedding walls, blocks. Healing will not be linear. It will not arrive one day in perfect form. It's a becoming. An unraveling. A putting together only to unspool a bit more. Stop trying to be "done" with the work of becoming yourself. Stop rushing it. You have a lifetime to master it. You're meant to have a lifetime to become, unfold, tense, and unfold again. It all belongs. It's all part of it. Maybe you need a break once in a while, but don't quit becoming truer versions of yourself. You don't have to become "better." Just truer. More you. More expressed. More free.

DAY 50

Imagine the person you want to be. Think of what their daily life, habits, and routines would be. Start showing up to those habits and routines, start building them, step by step, and day by day. You don't become them like magic. You *build* them. Start building.

DAY 51

They tell you if you aren't the absolute best at what you do, you're failing. If you're not always pushing and striving for more, *failing*. Make 6 figures! Make 7. Make 8! Be a billionaire! Dominate. Crush it. Have your first employee. Now have sixty. In a year! Otherwise—failing. Get promoted. Get promoted again. Be the last to leave, the first in. Never stop pushing. Never stop grinding. Work hard. Harder. Get it. You'll sleep when you're dead! Sleep, what's sleep? Weekends are for hustling. Midnights are for burning that oil. If you stop, your value plummets. If you take a breath, you might realize you want more exhales. You might realize you don't care about failing so much as *appearing* more successful. The pressure. The endless pressure. Be more. Do more. Share more. Hustle more. It never ends. It never ends... until you opt out. Build a life that is beautiful for you—and if being happy and joyful and calm and rested is failing, then so be it. May we all be such exquisite failures.

DAY 52

Knowing what you don't want to do is just as important as knowing what you do want to do. There is an overwhelm of choice. It's far too easy to get distracted by what other people are doing. Deciding when you definitely do not want to do something is crucial. Knowing what you don't care about and therefore do not need to spend mental energy thinking about is important information. Saying to yourself, this is not something I am interested in, opens up space for more of what does interest you. Listen when you don't care. File away that thing, that action, that impulse to keep up with whatever other people are doing. Save your mental energy. Protect your emotional space. Fill your time with what must get done to keep a life moving forward—and then fill the rest with joy and passion. Don't waste your time caring about things you don't care about. Be happy when you find something you don't care about that other people care about. One less thing to think about. Open space. Time. Freedom. This is what's valuable and you can give yourself more of it by being in tune with yourself and what you care about. What a gift.

DAY 53

Something really special happens when you say to yourself, *I'm still going to do what I set out to do and I'm going to do it my way, even if it takes longer than I've expected. Success on my own terms is more important than arbitrary timelines.* Because there is a very real magic that conspires to help you when you don't let doubt best you.

DAY 54

The heaviness will pass. You know by now that it always does. Just breathe. Sit with yourself. Try very hard not to take yourself out of what you need to learn here. There is so much to be gleaned from the heaviness, from the way it can feel like you're walking in slow motion, backwards. This kind of heaviness will ask you to give up on who you've imagined you can become. It will demand that you constrict, make your dreams and desires and needs a little smaller, a little more "realistic." But, do you want to be realistic? You are unrealistic and unprecedented and too multidimensional to be contained. Don't you know you're a galaxy? Don't you know the vast importance of yourself? I hope you never become realistic. That you never stop having wild hope. That you never let the current circumstances of your life determine the possibilities for your future. You cannot be contained. You cannot be labeled. You are you. And that matters. Even the heaviness wants to tell you: you're alive. You're alive. That matters.

DAY 55

The most useful skill is being able to do your work even as you doubt yourself. To show yourself that even if you don't have the confidence in yourself yet, you're still willing to do it. Waiting to feel confident, inspired, free of doubt and fear will have you waiting a long time. Learning to work even through emotional conditions that aren't ideal is how you build trust with yourself. And when you trust yourself implicitly, you become someone that *cannot* be discouraged.

DAY 56

Control suppresses your capacity to love. When you are controlling, you are not *experiencing*. Control can feel safe. If you keep it all together, nothing can fall apart. But sometimes things need to fall apart, so they can come back together stronger or built in new, better ways. When you are trying to control others, look at yourself: What, within you, is craving freedom? What are you clenching? Where do you need to let go? There is a beauty in relinquishing control. You allow it all to align in more awe-inspiring ways than you could imagine. You let what's not meant for you, completely miss you. When you stop controlling, you start allowing. And in the allowing, there is so much waiting for you. So much can line up in your best interest. So much can appear that you didn't notice before. So much can come together in ways you couldn't have predicted. Control is limiting. Stop grasping it all. Lay it down for a while. See where the flow of life takes you.

DAY 57

Deep down, you already know what you really want. All you have to do is give yourself permission to want it, make the decision to have it, and take even the smallest steps toward it. You owe yourself that.

DAY 58

You can't control what happens to you. This is true. The world can be random and you are often searching for meaning in senseless situations. But! You *can* control what you continue to allow. How what happened affected you. Your reaction. What you're going to make it mean about you moving forward. The boundary you set because of what happened. The standard you set to prevent it from happening again. The processing of the emotions from what happened. The sitting with the emotions and then the healing. The lessons, the meaning, the pain transmuted into something you can use, like acceptance. Not everything happens for a reason, but you can make a reason for everything. You can decide what happens next. You can write yourself a new story. You can set the boundary, call in something new. You can't control what happens to you, but don't give up the immense power of your own ability to heal, learn, and set new standards for what's allowed in your life.

DAY 59

You can be afraid and brave at the exact same time. Don't wait for perfect circumstances, perfect confidence, and the absence of doubt. You'll wait for too long. Be afraid and brave. Show up scared. Prove your courage in your actions. Confidence comes from the doing, the trying, the showing up—not from the perfection. Confidence builds by taking action in spite of the fear. Afraid and brave. *That's* the key.

DAY 60

I hope that you are truly rooted in why you do the things you do, why you wear the things you wear, why you spend your money the way you do, why you prioritize the people you do, why you do anything that takes up space in your mind. Are you living based on your own ideas and are your habits supporting you or diminishing you? Because, I hope you don't live your life on autopilot, doing the things other people do, and waiting for your time, hoping that things will change without ever trying to change them. The hours in your life belong to you. I hope you wake up a decade from now and feel that you lived based on your own wishes and desires and dreams. Because, no, you can't control everything. You can't decide everything that happens to you. You can't opt out of every responsibility. But, you can *seize* whatever choices you do have in your life and you can extract the most from them. You can take the empty space and fill it with joy, fill it with anything that brings you closer to that vision in your head of what you want your life to look like. You can do that. You can't have everything. You can't control everything. So, mold what you can. Choose what you can. And build a beautiful, intentional life around that.

DAY 61

Maybe boring is really good. Boring can mean healthy. Boring can mean happy. Boring can mean: you are no longer making a mess of your own life just to feel interesting. Maybe boring is the start of it all, of letting go of external expectations, and coming home to you.

DAY 62

Even if you're not exactly where you want to be, live your life with the wild freedom you're reserving for that moment. What are you waiting for? Seriously, what are you waiting for? Are you truly working toward a big goal that is requiring all your time and focus? Or are you using that goal as a way to keep yourself from living your life? Because I have to tell you: there never comes a moment where all the goals are complete, everything is perfect, and it all lines up. That moment is not coming to tell you to go enjoy your life. You have to decide. You have to choose. Today you will prioritize your joy. Today you will look on the optimistic side. Today you will let go and be in the moment. You can do that. It's in your power to decide what you will focus on. And the more you focus on your joy, the more it expands in your life. The more you focus on what's working, the more you'll see how it's all working out for you. Your focus amplifies anything. So make sure you focus on what you're *building*, not on what you're leaving behind.

DAY 63

So much becomes easier when you trust yourself. You listen within instead of getting cues from societal expectations. You make easier decisions from a place of conviction. You allow yourself to contain more joy, happiness, and excitement since you know you can trust yourself to weather the "opposite" of those emotions. You feel safer with yourself. And you become a soft place to land. Before the self-love and self-care, there needs to be self-trust. It's very hard to love and care for someone you don't trust. And that includes the relationship you have with yourself. Trust is the foundation. When you trust yourself, you hold yourself. You don't lose yourself. You know when you need to pull back to rest or when you need to push a little further. You can be still, calm in a frantic, loud world. Build your own trust and see what comes together and falls apart. Whatever happens, you trust yourself to know what to do. *That* is power.

DAY 64

If you give yourself an endless supply of compassion as you pursue your goals, compassion will follow you everywhere. If you berate yourself into achievement, you will berate yourself whether you're striving or at the top. How you get there is how you are when you arrive. If you *start* with compassion, you *arrive* with compassion. Compassion gets you there with joy. Berating gets you there with perpetual dissatisfaction. It's up to you which motivation you choose.

DAY 65

Find a way to love your life so much that you feel lucky to be you. Like it's a privilege just to wake up as yourself. Like you are utterly charmed by your own life. What a beautiful home you've built. What incredible friends you get to text all day. How you spend your time and your life—genius. What fun! What a strong mind you have. What a way you care for yourself and listen to your needs. What great kids or dogs or cats or plants you've raised. Wow, you've got this whole life thing figured out. Or, if not, look at you, trying to figure it out and fight for your joy. How lucky you are that you get to be you.

DAY 66

How do you change? You draw a line in the sand and refuse to harm yourself any longer. You stop saying unkind words to yourself, thinking it will motivate you. You stop doing things on a daily basis that you know don't make you feel good. You find a way to keep your promises to yourself. You make smaller promises. Or you put your promises in your schedule, circle them in red pen. You make yourself non-negotiable. You make feeling good your priority. You change your mind on what you believe you deserve. You heal toward a more freer version of yourself. You stop paying attention to people who make you feel like the gap between where you are and where you want to be is too large. You treat yourself delicately. You listen to how you feel because trust is about listening. You make a vow to yourself that you will feel good, that you will no longer be your own worst enemy—and you do whatever you can to keep that vow. You make yourself matter. And you heal. You heal so you can be free.

DAY 67

It's not just "choose happiness." That's too simplistic. It's more like: You can choose to see the lessons coming through for you. You can choose to make meaning out of your experiences. You can choose to find a slice of delight in your day. You can choose how you interpret what happens to you, what you make it mean. You can choose to be compassionate, kind, and forgiving toward yourself. You can choose who you listen to, whose voices you give space and attention to. You can choose where you put your energy. You can choose to tear yourself down or build yourself up. You can choose to seek answers, solutions, help, when you feel you have no other choices. You can choose how you let your past affect your present, what stories and narratives about yourself you cling to or unlearn. You can choose what habits you add into your day. You can choose to see yourself as "not there yet" or as a wonderful ever-evolving work in progress. You can choose the filter you view your life through. You can choose to see the unbelievable power of claiming your choices and agency. Right now. *Today.*

DAY 68

It's not that you're lost; it's that you're growing into someone who is prepared for what's next. It's not that you don't know what you want; it's that your intuition wants to be heard. It's not that you're falling behind; it's that you're being reminded that focusing on your own path is far more important than trying to measure up. It's not that you doubt yourself; it's that you're out on the ledge, taking risks, being bold, and with that comes uncertainty. Doubt is a sign of courage. It's not that you haven't done enough; it's that you need to celebrate all your small steps and small wins. You are always doing so much better than you think. Shift your attention, listen to your intuition, follow the ease and joy—and you'll see it all clearly again.

DAY 69

So much of your life is *unexplainable*. Why the timing always seems to make sense. Why you gravitate to certain people and not others. Why something you want to happen so badly, doesn't, only to come back around exactly when you were about to give up. There is so much magic in this world that cannot be explained. You are part of the magic. Your life is an experiment. Uncertainty is part of this adventure. The journey you're on is asking for your trust. Trust in timing. In yourself. In the unfolding. Embrace that you're not meant to know the whole plan. Embrace the surprises and detours. Maybe the detour you are fighting against is about to open up a whole new world for you. Maybe the timing you can't trust is going to bring you exactly what you desire when you're most ready to receive it. Maybe there is so much more here that cannot be rationalized. The magic of your own life becomes so beautifully apparent when you start noticing it. So, fix your eyes there. Notice how life continues to delight and surprise you.

DAY 70

Self-doubt is proof of bravery. If you stayed in one place, and never tried anything new ever again, there would be nothing to fear. But where's the fun in that? Self-doubt is the bridge between where you are and where you're going. Bravery doesn't feel like bravery when you're in it. It feels like fear, an uncertain and raw vulnerability. It is only in retrospect that you see that the bridge you've just crossed had so much intrinsic value. But, taking the first step across the bridge, it's not always comfortable. *That's okay.* You came here to learn, to grow, to evolve, and to actualize all the many things that are on your heart. Love your self-doubt. It is proof you are trying, that you are vulnerable, that you are doing something uncertain and bold. Your self-doubt is a badge of honor. It's you braving the wild unknown and letting yourself be changed by the journey. It's you stepping out of the ordinary, and into something extraordinary, simply by being a person who does not give in to fear. Self-doubt is proof you care deeply and what a beautiful and wonderful thing that is.

DAY 71

It's all going to be okay. Take a breath. Take a break. Whatever you're churning around in your mind right now can wait. Surrender it. Let it go. Have an ice cream. Go on a walk. Whatever you're trying to figure out will be *figured out*. You just need to let the answers get to you, and it's real hard to do that if your mind is filled with questions. Let it go. Leave an open space for the next step to appear.

DAY 72

You need to learn how to know yourself. Your life will exist in phases and seasons. Sometimes you won't be clear on what you want, and you'll need to figure out ways to connect to what is true and still within. Sometimes you'll know exactly what you want, and you'll need to figure out ways to bring it all to fruition, to honor your desires and dreams. You will not stay the same. This is the truth. You will be in constant flux and you need to understand how to meet yourself where you are. Knowing yourself cannot be outsourced. It is a lifelong journey. You will always be with you. It's important work to cultivate a relationship with yourself built on honesty. Who are you really? Who are you when nobody is looking? Do you know how to access your gifts and genius? Do you know how to come back to yourself after a period of disconnection? Your body and your soul are always trying to get your attention. Don't get busy building someone else's version of a beautiful life. Find out what *yours* is. Build that version. Build your beautiful life. Starting within.

DAY 73

So, *be alone*. Learn the shape of yourself. Sit with the pain of your past and breathe it into the air; tell the truth to yourself and find forgiveness there. It's time you learn to rely on yourself, to be able to find stillness in solitude, to not reach for the nearest distraction when you're almost there, almost to the core of you, peeled back and vulnerable. It's time you stop being afraid of yourself, of what your thoughts might conjure up when it's quiet and just you and you. It's time you stop using things and people to feed your avoidance. It's time you remember that the relationship you have with yourself requires as much care and time as the relationships you have with others. Everything in life gets better—more precious and more important—when you love yourself alone, when you are not afraid of being on your own, when you can sit with your shadow and acknowledge it, listen, and not let it affect you. Everything is easier when you love your own company. Because it finally means everyone and everything in your life is there by intentional choice—not need, not escapism, not avoidance. A lovely choice. A calm choice. And isn't that just so much better?

DAY 74

There comes a time when you must stop talking about all the things you want to be doing and just... start doing them. Action cures fear. Get started on something even if it's for ten minutes per day. The only way to know what you most want is to get the idea out of your head and *begin*.

DAY 75

Here's something truly radical: Even if it's not perfect, even if it doesn't look like how you thought it would, even if you have hard days and bad days, even if sometimes you wish you'd chosen differently, even if it's not trendy or cool or aspirational to other people, even if it's a little frantic and chaotic and messy, even if all this is true and more... you can *still* love yourself and your life.

DAY 76

There is no time limit on your potential. There is no clock
above you counting down the days until your irrelevance.
This society wants to tell you who gets to be important and
special. It can break a spirit. It can count you out before
you've even had a shot. But here's the secret: you don't have
to listen to them. You don't have to subscribe to their expectations. You can completely and totally and radically opt
out. That is your choice. You can believe them or you can
not. It's easier said than done, but it's harder to believe them.
It's harder to live by their rules. It's harder to deny yourself
and put yourself on an impossible timeline. You have time.
You can always start over. You can always decide on who you
are and refuse to be put in a box. That is *your* choice. That
is your power. Will you wield it? More than staying in the
lines, this society needs you limitless and fully expressed.

DAY 77

Have the courage to change your mind. To change directions. To throw out what feels okay to what lights you up. Start doing the thing that you think about when you're on the couch or trying to go to sleep. Start doing the thing you've been avoiding. Do an hour a day. Carve out the time with a machete. Say "no" more. Don't compromise on what you want. You may need to be patient. You may need to acquire some skills. You may have your commitment tested. But don't compromise on yourself. Shift, evolve, grow. Let yourself be tugged in the direction of what brings you the most joy.

JAMIE VARON

DAY 78

Your life doesn't have to be shiny and glittery and exciting
to be interesting. The way you exist can be poetry. How you
take a moment with your coffee in the morning. The way
you laugh when you read a good book. The way you cook
a simple meal with devotion. The way you do your life and
be in your life. It can be art. It can be simple and it can be
interesting and you don't need to reinvent the entirety of
your identity to realize that you are really cool, even with
your quirks and your routines and your boundaries and your
no's and your yes's and the things you pay attention to and
the details you care about and the passion you have that is
fierce and fiery that nobody else has, not like you, not in the
way you have it. Your life can be small by choice. You can
settle down and build a little home and have a few plants,
maybe a dog, and the interesting part will never be the big,
shiny moments. It will always be the way you figure out how
to live, how to carve out long stretches of joy, how to make
peace with all of the world's contradictions, and how to find
a place of your own, throw a stake down, and claim, *mine.*
Mine. Mine. Mine.

DAY 79

You are not required to please anyone but yourself. It does not matter what other people think about your choices, because they do not have to *live out* your choices every day. Your life belongs to you entirely. And, spending this one life of yours trying to collect enough approval from others to finally approve of yourself is a waste of time. Focus on making your life exactly the way you want it to be that you naturally and organically do not care at all about what other people think of how you live. Do you so well that you don't have time to do anything but be alive in your own life.

DAY 80

Your life is allowed to be enjoyable. People sometimes forget this. They do exercise they don't enjoy to get a certain type of body. They do work they dislike to get a certain type of lifestyle. They are so often sacrificing their joy for some societal goals they're *supposed* to want. And yet, their joy, their enjoyment, their love of their own life—how is that not the standard for well-being? Too many people have normalized that their life is only as good as it looks to others. This requires ignoring your inner knowing, the most vital truth you have at your disposal. It's why people hustle. It's why they obsess over hard work as opposed to inspired effort. It might explain why they are exhausted, and yet unfulfilled and burnt out. Because there is a knowing within all of them—a map that will lead them to what is most true. Success is not some external guidepost. It has always been within—how you feel about yourself, the life you're building, and the amount of joy, calm, happiness, and love you allow yourself to contain. Success is not out there. It's about creating a life you love so much that feels so true to you, you have nothing left to prove.

DAY 81

Here's how it goes: You will figure it all out only to get lost again. You will heal and learn and then you will heal and relearn. You will change and think you will be that way forever and then you will reinvent. You will never be "done" and that is the whole point. You will grow and then you will savor. You will be sad and then you will be blissful, sometimes in the same twenty-four hours. You will cry. You will compare and then you will recommit to your truth. You will get caught up in societal expectations and then you will find your connection to self again. You will be in constant evolvement, some of it conscious, most of it happening in the background. You will meet new versions of yourself all the time if you're lucky, if you're present enough to invite them in. You will think you have all the answers and then you will be humbled by all you do not know yet. You will follow a path only to realize you need an entirely new North Star. And all of this will be okay and serve to remind you that you're *wonderfully* alive to your life.

DAY 82

Find a way to fall in love with your life so intensely that watching another person love theirs is a confirmation, not a threat. Be so involved with cultivating your own talents and forging through your own desires that you don't have the time or energy to criticize how others live. Determine for yourself what matters to you, how you want to experience life, and let that, and only that, be your map. *Stop letting other people's lives be your map.* Let yourself want what you want and be patient, let it unfold, see what's right in front of you, and listen to your wild urges, to your painful jealousies, to the what if's and why not me's, and reach, small step by small step, until you can't remember when you ever felt anything but wholly in love with the life you've created.

DAY 83

You can change your mind. You can set new intentions. You can decide how you show up even to the hard parts of life. You can rewrite your own narrative. You can unlearn stories that are harmful to you. Stop believing it's not within your power to transform. Stop believing you are not capable of magical change. Don't let that power sit within you, unable to be expressed. Who you are right now is not who you have to continue to be. Who you were in the past is a version of you that can stay there. There is so many more possibilities available to you in your future. Trust that you are allowed to become many different iterations of yourself. Trust that you can change. Trust that your life is not meant to be stagnant. You are going somewhere beautiful. All you need to do is start believing that you are—and act accordingly.

DAY 84

Believe in your own potential. You are capable of great transformations. You have become so many versions of yourself over the years. There is still so much more for you to discover about yourself. Do not give up on you. Let your dreams shift and change. Let your ambitions rise and fall. But don't stop believing in your capacity for growth. It is not time for you to whittle your desires down to regrets. Experiment. Shift. Pivot. Be flexible in your identity. This world can be very difficult, but please don't be your own biggest barrier. Do not be the person who tells you that you can't do it, or it's too late, or you're too old. You can do it. It's not too late. And age does not tell you what's possible for you. Wherever you are now, you can be in a totally different place a month, a year from now. So much can change when you stay *open*. When you stay hopeful. Stop resisting life and the changes it wants from you. Let life take you on the tide for a while. See where you go. See all that is available for you when you're open to a transformation.

DAY 85

Do things for yourself, because you just want to see how far you can go. Grow, because you can't wait to meet new versions of yourself. Remember that your life is meant to *delight* you. Let yourself be delighted, by your own gifts and talents and unique interests and hobbies that stay on your mind. You are you for a reason. Find the many reasons. Keep your own interests alive. Don't let your own fire go out. Take pleasure in the way you do certain things, the situations that make you angry, that bring you to passion. Make sure you are heart-first in whatever you do. Trust that your efforts will add up to something unexpected and wonderful. Let life surprise you. If something doesn't happen for you, trust that it's not meant for you and the reasons will appear when you most need them. Take delight in your own path. Heal so you can be free. Forget being the "best" or having the "most." Be you. That is enough. More than enough. Enjoy who you are. There is nobody like you and that is delightful. Let yourself bask in that for a while.

DAY 86

At some point, you decide. You decide that *this* is where you are rooted. You make the decision to be happy, right where you are. You don't let go of your dreams, but you let yourself make new dreams. You expand your dreams. You decide that this is where you plant, this is where you take root, this is where you will bloom. You don't wait for it all to be perfect. You construct the life that feels beautiful and wonderful and generative right where you are. You get to decide that. You look around and pause to feel gratitude for what you have already created. You let in simple joys, easy pleasures. You take up a hobby. You stop forcing so much. You let go of control. You look at the raw materials of your life and you go, "I can make something extraordinary with this." And you start to build, right from where you're planted. You don't wait for it all to line up. You line it all up yourself, brick by brick.

DAY 87

Yes, you were made for more. But maybe it's not about more tasks. More work. More responsibility. More consumption. More money. Or more conventional success. Ever think that, instead, you were made for more laughter? More spontaneous fun. More sunshine on your face. More ice cream. More feeling at home in your body. More swims in the ocean, free, limbs exposed to the open air. More love. More long, lingering dinners with conversations that take on inspiring, thought-provoking tangents. More deep talks. More depth, in general. More days lost in a book or a life. More smiling. More joy. More warm evenings that are punctuated with contentment. More sighs of relief. More pasta. More bread. More food that you love without one moment of guilt. More hugs. More of that feeling you get when you are hooked on a new book and feel ravenous to finish it. *More of life.* More of you being exactly you. More enjoying. So much more of the enjoying.

DAY 88

Build a life that makes you smile, in the simplest moments, even if that kind of life doesn't look splashy on the internet. Make choices that make you feel lighter, even if those choices don't reflect what society has told you that you "should" do. Befriend people you respect, who inspire you, even if it means starting over. Interpret your life through the lens of positivity and optimism, even in a world that is harsh and insensitive. Orient yourself in the direction of joy, every single day. Focus on what's *working* in your life. Give more space to "it's all working out for me" to be true for you. Hope is not dangerous. It's essential. Be your own support system. Make your mind into a beautiful garden, where you can choose the most beautiful thought at any given time. No one deserves a life they love more than you. But you do need to create it, build it, curate it. You do need to trust yourself. You do need to let go of how you think it should be, and find out who you are, what your opinion is, what matters most to you. Know yourself. Choose yourself. Love yourself. Let your life expand.

DAY 89

All that really matters in life is feeling good, is being alive to your life while you have it. There is always going to be hardship, or circumstances outside of your control, or unwieldy emotions, or demands on your time and attention. But you must not wait for life to slow down before you slow it all down. You must demand that it does. You must carve out little pockets of joy in your ordinary days. You must learn to rest without feeling guilt about resting. It's so important to know what makes you feel good, to know what you must do each day to keep yourself feeling well. You must stop glamorizing neglecting your well-being as a sacrifice for more achievement, to consume more, to have more, to be insatiable. You must recognize that life is happening now whether you're noticing it or not. And if you don't take time out of the frantic nature of life to stop, pause, enjoy, savor, slow down—then a day becomes a week becomes a month becomes a whole life—*missed*. Notice your life. Be alive to it all. Stop waiting for the savoring. You've done enough. Enjoy it for a while.

DAY 90

There are so many ways to live a life. Try some people on. Take risks. Reinvent yourself. What is the point in staying the same? Surround yourself with people who support your growth. Grow so much you don't recognize yourself in a year. This is your life. Yours. It's wonderful to be thoughtful to others, but you don't need to cramp down to appease them. There's a difference in being generous as opposed to being a martyr. Nobody deserves a beautiful life more than you. Don't cut yourself off from your desire, and joy. And if you ever do, find a way to come home to yourself. You're allowed to dream. You're allowed to pursue. It might be slow. You may need to carve out pockets of stolen time. But you are allowed to reinvent yourself. Become many versions of yourself. Blossom and bloom. Stand up to your full height. You are not the supporting character in someone else's story. You're the lead. *Take it.*

DAY 91

Ask yourself: Who do I want to be a year from now? Not what do you want to be or what do you want to do. What kind of *person* do you want to be? Do you want to be someone who hardens in the face of adversity or someone who softens from it, who learns from it, whose compassion deepens from it? Do you want to be someone who listens within and takes their cues from their intuition? Do you want to be in love with your life? Forget the perfect job, the perfect person, having it all lined up. Who do you want to be? Make a map to become that person. Put in the daily steps. Build that life. Don't wait for all the perfect scenarios to line up. Have a vision. Build that beautiful vision in small steps and don't let it out of your sight.

DAY 92

Your self-belief will take you further than anything else. You have to be a little obsessed with your vision. You have to believe in yourself almost to a delusional degree. There's always going to be reasons to give up. Always something that seems more important to spend your time doing. You will be surrounded by naysayers. Encouragement is not the way of this world. There's a million reasons not to try. Not everyone is going to see what you see. Not everyone understands what you've got in your daydream. You don't need anything other than your self-belief. You have to see what others can't see. You have to know you are capable. You have to be undaunted by setbacks. It doesn't matter what you want to do, but the way you do it. The way you approach it. When you've got your self-belief locked in, that is going to carry you through the ups and downs that are inevitable. You can't control anything outside of yourself but when you've got the steadiness of self-belief on your side, you don't really need everything to go your way. *You're* the way.

DAY 93

Nobody knows you better than you know yourself. Nobody can tell you what your intuition is whispering to you. Nobody can tell you what lights you up, what makes you excited in the morning, what brings you the most joy. This is a loud world with a lot of opinions, but please remember that, whatever you do, you're the one that has to live your life. Make sure you've allowed yourself some solitude and space to know who you are. In a world of trends, sameness, and conformity, be your truest self. There's a reason you're here and I hope you let yourself discover it, instead of letting external pressure tell you what to love and who to be.

DAY 94

Love is not the opposite of fear. It's not fear or love. It's fear or trust. You either stoke fear in yourself by believing in your inadequacy, insecurity, or lack of readiness. Or, you surrender entirely to the trust that you never have to be perfect, you only have to be present and keep showing up and following where you are being led. The belief that you must be "good enough" to have the life you want is false. The belief itself is causing the suffering, not any evidence you think you have against yourself. The belief that you aren't "ready" yet is the source of your suffering. You are putting your life on hold. You are creating a wall between you and your life. The belief in fear creates this wall. It is constructed entirely in your mind. Because when you put your trust into the flow of your life, the wall disappears. The suffering ends. Absolutely nothing outside of you could have changed and suddenly you are at peace. Why don't you trust that peaceful feeling? Because you think life demands your suffering. Because you think your fear is more real than your trust. It's not. It's either fear or trust. Those are your only two choices. Which path will you embark on today?

DAY 95

It's the simplest things—the rituals you keep, the way you speak to yourself, how you react to the unexpected—that determines your quality of life. It's not how impressive you can make your life seem to others. It's the way you can extract lessons and growth from even the most challenging situations. It's not how many friends you have but how many friends you actually connect with, who see the truth of you. The simplest things can often be the hardest in a world that has told us simplicity isn't enough. Your joy is found in true, grounded gratitude. It's found in respecting, showing up for, and being honest with yourself. It's found in listening to your emotions instead of busying yourself out of them. You may think you have to *earn* your well-being, but it's always available to you. Don't mistake the world's definition of a "good life" for your own, for the simplicity of what truly matters to you. This world will have you chasing down so much that doesn't matter. When you can access joy in the simplicity of life, everything becomes more magical.

DAY 96

One of the kindest things you can do for others is to show your effort. No, you didn't just wake up like that. No, it didn't all just come together effortlessly. You worked hard and put in the time and agonizingly combed through limiting beliefs and had to use the force of will to show up, day in, day out. Make the unseen work, seen, so that nobody thinks some of the hardest things in life can be reduced to easy, effortless solutions when they almost never are. Get into the details. What did it take? What did you have to heal? What did you do in the dark night of the soul in order to emerge into this version of yourself? Show the effort. Normalize the reality that life is often a lot of behind the scenes tedious work and the highlight reel is never the full story. Almost nothing is effortless. It's a ruse and a myth. Behind the effortlessness is where all the real alchemy is happening, anyway.

DAY 97

You must believe so deeply in yourself that no amount of rejection or success can topple you. You must put your head down when nobody is clapping for you and keep going anyway. What you do in the silence and stillness will carry you through the waves of recognition. One moment you're on top, the next you're ignored. It's all part of it. But when you have self-belief, nothing brings you down for long. You believe in yourself, *regardless*. That is true power in a world intent on making you desperate for external validation. Someone who doesn't need that validation is a very potent type of person.

DAY 98

The truth is, sometimes you'll need to rest and sometimes you'll need to keep yourself accountable to the promises you made to you. Sometimes you'll need to pull back and sometimes you'll need to remind yourself of your own resolve. Sometimes doing nothing feels best. Sometimes being productive does. Sometimes even the best things for you will be uncomfortable and difficult. Sometimes they will approach with ease. Sometimes you'll have a year of planting seeds. Sometimes you'll have the year of harvest. Sometimes you need to be gentle with yourself. And sometimes you need some tough love. Sometimes it's a them problem. And sometimes it's a you problem. Sometimes you have to listen to your intuition. And sometimes you have to listen to your logic. Resist the urge to exist on a binary and live in the extremes. The best thing you could ever do is learn to intimately know yourself. You are nuanced. You are complex. Nobody knows you better than you. If you take anything with you into right now, take that.

DAY 99

Like yourself first. Choose yourself first. Learn to be alone with the shape of yourself. Validate your feelings. Tell the truth to yourself above all. When you are your own fiercest advocate, you can make easier, more aligned decisions. You don't go searching for your worth in places you won't find it. You don't hustle and strive, hoping to prove yourself to an invisible audience of people you think can give you what you have to give yourself. Love yourself first. Do the work. Get deep. Get deeper. Heal. Get curious with yourself. Get quiet. Get still. Everything that's meant for you can come right in when you know who you are and what doesn't belong in your space. When you choose yourself first, you don't wait to be chosen. And when you're a person who is no longer waiting to be chosen, your life opens up in formidable ways.

DAY 100

You've spent enough time figuring out how to prepare for the worst. Maybe, see what it's like if you prepare for your own success, no matter what it is you want to do. Start asking more interesting questions beyond what can go wrong and what if this doesn't work out. What about these questions instead: How many different ways can this work out? How good can it get? What's working in my favor? Where is the light and where is it directing me? Where is the warmth? When you are constantly shutting down possibilities, all you'll see are obstacles. But when you start asking *expansive* questions, what you're going to get are possibilities. The road opens up, finally. There are answers. There are new directions. New paths. And when you can finally see the fog clear, you can move forward. That clarity very often comes down to asking better questions.

DAY 101

The bad news is that there will never be a time when your life is totally perfect or when nobody in the world is suffering. This time will never arrive. There is never a "right time" for your joy. The permission to feel it will never come, if what you're waiting for is permission. The good news is that because there is never a right time to fully succumb to joy, it means all the time is the right time. Just think of all the bounty around you. Fresh melons dripping with sweetness. A tomato so plump you could eat it whole. A peach so juicy you declare it your favorite fruit. Bodies of water on hot days. A cool shower after a day at the pool, your skin warm from the sun. Ice cream on a humid evening. Two minute hugs. An infinite number of galaxies that puts your life into perspective. There is never a right time for joy. So that means, you must succumb to it whenever it's available. Don't deny it, waiting for perfect circumstances that'll never arrive. Succumb. There is so much here for you to discover.

DAY 102

Instead of focusing on how much more you have left to do, take a deep breath and recognize just how far you've come. There are parts of you that don't ache the same way they used to. There are people you no longer miss. Situations that no longer bring you to your knees. There are things you do now, easily, that used to feel impossible. Yes, it's important to keep moving forward but it's equally important to see the distance you've traveled, the versions of yourself you thought you'd never outgrow that are but distant memories now. It's incredible, just how much you have healed, traversed, let go, and accomplished. Progress is amazing, but take a moment to acknowledge just how much ground you've *already* covered. Breathe that in. Sit there for today.

DAY 103

Your purpose is not something you discover one day, possess it, and that's it. Your purpose is an ever-evolving byproduct of living by your own intuition. Expect your purpose to change. Expect to discover new aspects of yourself that feel meaningful and purposeful. You're not done. The minute you think you've figured it all out, that's when you're at the bottom of a new mountain, waiting to climb. You can stay there, make camp, and ignore all your longings to begin the ascent. Or you can see life as an unfolding adventure, your purpose shifting and growing and changing because you are the one shifting, growing, and changing. The trick is not to see that mountain as a block, but as an exciting new challenge for you to apply all your past lessons and insights onto. The only way you can ever know your strength is by starting the climb, and seeing just how far you can go now.

DAY 104

Eventually, this will all make sense. You'll know why you were held back, why it didn't come together, why you felt blocked or lost or uncertain or frustrated. One day, you'll see the thread leading you to where you're going. One day, you'll find yourself in the middle of a life you never expected to have and you'll be happy for what didn't come to fruition for you. You'll be grateful you were spared of a life that wasn't going to be best for you. One day, you'll look back on right now and be glad you didn't pack it in and give up. One day, the parts of you that you might not understand will have a deep and unmistakable purpose. One day, you'll be able to see the magic in how it all unfolded for you. You'll understand how you were tasked to grow into the person who could receive the kind of life you're asking for. One day, all the hard days, healing, and time spent trying to understand yourself—it will have led you to something so beautiful, so perfect for you, that it'll all click in. *Oh, this is why.* This is where I didn't know I was going all along.

DAY 105

You don't need to be selfless. You're not a martyr. You're allowed to make your life a symphony. You're allowed to be heavily invested in your own life. You're allowed a life that feels really good to you. Without explanation. Without condition. *You're allowed.*

DAY 106

Listening to yourself takes an immense amount of courage. Nobody talks about this enough. The world is so loud. It'll tell you exactly how to be, how to look, how to exist, how to work, how to be good, how to be bad, how to do anything and everything. What it won't do is encourage you to listen to whatever feels right and true and light and warm within you. It's the hardest thing, to find a slice of solitude quiet enough for you to hear your own needs, wants, desires, thoughts. It takes so much bravery and self-trust to follow what feels true instead of what you "should" do. It's brave to grow when the world seems to want you to conform. It's brave to do what feels right to you when it seems like everyone else is going in the opposite direction. It's rebellion. It's going against the tide, the status quo. And I want to commend you for doing it. Because it's hard. Sometimes it's lonely. But most of all, it's intensely rewarding. A lot of the bravest things usually are.

DAY 107

If not getting something makes you question whether you deserve it or not, you're still not ready to receive it. Read that again. If a "failure" is proof to you that you're not good enough, then you still don't have unshakable self-belief. You're still not trusting. You're still doubting. If something doesn't go the way you expect and you are at peace, knowing that a rejection is a divine redirection and any perceived failure is a rewarding part of the process, you're good. When you are content in your path and your timing, then you're ready. When you don't need the blessings to know you're already blessed, it's time. Just hold on and stay prepared.

DAY 108

Love yourself in action. You can stare at the mirror and repeat words of love to yourself all you want but maybe there's a better way. Maybe you need to love yourself differently. Think of the relationship you have with yourself like any other relationship. It needs to build. Listen to yourself. Care for yourself. Figure out what you need—and then give yourself that. Feel your emotions. Cultivate trust with yourself. The love cannot just be in words alone. There needs to be loving *actions*. Trust being secured. Tenderness and intimacy. Compassion. Nourishment and forgiveness. You need to show yourself love, act in loving ways, and build a solid relationship with you.

DAY 109

There is a false belief that if you aren't hard on yourself, that's giving up. There's a sort of fear of self-love, that it will make you lazy or too soft. And this is rooted in the belief that your output and productivity is your only value in society. So the more you withhold your own love, thinking you must earn it, the less connected you become to your gentleness, and joy, and calm, and satisfaction, and contentment. But it's a myth. Your own love will not lead you down harmful paths. You own love is the power. You own love will be so catalyzing it has you showing up for yourself in ways that you could never expect. Your own love will make you gentle and maybe it will make you soft, but it's only a broken society that tells you those things are not valuable. To be closed down and robotic is easy. To be soft is difficult. It takes courage and strength. To be gentle in a culture that wants you to be a machine with no needs—what a revelation. To stay open to growth, to feel your feelings, to love yourself in a world that makes it so hard—*that* is the work. That is the work that has the most value.

DAY 110

You are not required to be your own worst enemy. The less you pick fights with yourself, the less your life will feel like a battle. You've done that for a long time—being hard on yourself. Try being light on yourself. See how that goes for a bit. Be good to you. It might just unlock a whole new uplevel for you. You never know. Try it and see.

DAY III

One of the most important things is to allow yourself to change over the years. Who you were is not who you have to continue being. Discovering new passions and new dreams and new hobbies and new excitements and new little breadcrumbs that lead you to more fulfillment is part of the journey. You are never frozen in place. You are never meant to be one person and just stay that way forever. Being open to the ways you evolve is such a beautiful experience. You are always discovering new things. You are willing to experiment. You are open to being someone you haven't been before. Life is short, but the days can be long. The months. The years. Don't get too comfortable being exactly who you've always been that you don't let yourself change, grow, and evolve. Reinvention is probably one of life's sweetest gifts.

DAY 112

The problem is that you think confidence is something that is bestowed upon you. When you achieve enough or get promoted to the right title or have the right education or garner enough acclaim or popularity or when someone else, somewhere else, awards you the right to believe in yourself. You keep waiting for permission. You keep waiting for proof. And when you get "proof" it doesn't feel like "enough." So, you need another goal. You think, once you achieve that one, you'll have permission to be confident. But that's not how it works. It never feels like enough because it actually isn't. If you don't feel it inside, you don't know how to receive it outside of you either. Your innate confidence, built by doing what is truest to you and following your path, is what magnetizes everything to you. So much so that once you get it "all" you'll realize you don't even need it anymore.

DAY 113

Growth can be scary. It can be wonderful. It can be exciting. And it can be terrifying. You're going somewhere you've never been before. You're becoming a version of yourself that has never existed. This is why people resist change and growth so often. It's stepping into the unknown. It's trusting that there is something vital on the other side. It's an act of faith to continue to grow and evolve. You are boldly going forward into chapters you haven't read yet. You are writing your story as you go. There is no control. No predictability. No safety. No comfort zone. When you grow, you leap forward, trusting the next step will appear. So yeah, if growth and change makes you afraid, that means you're doing it right. You are in the darkness between where you've been and where you're going. Trust it. Stumble forward. You're courageously becoming someone you haven't been yet.

DAY 114

Sometimes when you're following your own path, when you're blazing your own trail, it might take a while for the world to catch up to you. You might look at the well-worn path others have taken and thought—maybe that's what I should do. But instead you keep going through the dark thicket of your own. You make your way. You clear out the debris. You try to do it differently. And maybe your path is more winding. Maybe it's a little slower. Maybe you would have gotten "there" faster if you followed everyone else. But you have something even more precious. You have *your* way. Whatever you gain, belongs to you. You aren't living someone else's life and calling it enough. You stayed true to yourself. And at the end of the day, isn't that the real success?

DAY 115

What if you don't need a plan? What if you let go of how you think it should all work out and let it unfold even better than you could imagine? What if you stopped clenching on to what you think will make you happy one day and instead cultivate happiness in your everyday life? What if you stopped hoarding your joy and celebrations for when you're "good enough" and instead started celebrating every single tiny step of progress? What if you got super clear on what makes you excited and just kept saying yes to that feeling? What if you don't need to have it all figured out? Not today? Not in the future? Not ever? What if you just keep going to the next right thing and trusted that it's all coming together for you? What if you trusted that if you let go and breathe a little, you can receive so much more of what you most want? What if you let yourself flow with life? What if that's when all the gifts, magic, and surprises can finally get to you? What if? What if? What if?

DAY 114

Be an active participant in your life. Believe in
change. Believe that a month, a year can change
anything. Believe in new beginnings. Believe
in fresh starts. Believe in healing through and
beyond. You are not your past. You are not
your current circumstances. Believe in *renewal*.

DAY 117

Over the years, maybe your dreams change. Actually, maybe they change and shift and expand. You start to realize that life is pretty long and if you don't keep adding in new dreams, there's not a whole lot to wake up for in the morning. Maybe you realize you don't have this one thing that makes you happy but instead a collection of little and big joys. You realize your life could include a whole tapestry of dreams. A kaleidoscope. Maybe you even give one of your big dreams a try. You realize maybe it's not about getting the glory, but just being devoted to the dream. Being on the path of listening within and extracting the next steps. The dream isn't really about the destination, but the joy contained within the wondering, the wandering, the doing, and the trying. The point of any dream is to get you up and in your life, engaged with it. And wherever that takes you, make it beautiful, because you built that by your own excitement, following one light after another.

DAY 118

Don't let fear make your decisions for you. Expect the unexpected. Feel lucky. Keep fighting for joy. Because, at the end of this long and yet somehow short life of yours, you're going to want to know, without doubt, that every day, every month, every year that you were privileged enough to be alive that you fought for joy and you looked in both ordinary and extraordinary moments for the magic in it all.

DAY 119

Disappointment stems from the expectation that it should have gone differently, instead of the way it went. But, how do you know? You try to know by measuring—well, someone else seems better than me and got it instead. That's the story you tell yourself. But expectations are illusions you create in your mind to measure whether you are doing "well" or not. Expectations are pure projection, crafted from comparing your journey to someone else's. So, what if you let it be? What if you trusted that what has shown up in your life is your soul's journey? What if you stopped assuming someone else has it "better" than you and instead, saw what was here for you, right now, even now, even in the middle of all this? How would your life change if you radically trusted that you are exactly where you're meant to be? Would you enjoy the present more? Would you enjoy *yourself* more? Would all the space you've crammed with expectations instead fill with excitement, anticipation, freedom? Let go. Be for a while. Trust that everything is conspiring in your favor.

DAY 120

Your life isn't always outside your comfort zone. You don't have to take big risks and light your life on fire to feel alive. You don't have to be uncomfortable every second of every day in order to be "successful." You can seek stability. You can learn the ways of feeling safe within your body. You can work toward the noble goal of uncovering the simple pleasures of your life before they told you those weren't big enough. Finding a way to feel calm in a frenzied, frantic world is a big goal. Finding a way to breathe through anxiety in a more, better, faster world is not easy. Finding a way to feel stable in an uncertain world is not a "small life." You might be risking even more by trying to make your life so big and impressive. You might work so hard to never settle, never make your life small, never let good enough be enough that you miss everything worth living for. Small joys. Simple pleasures. Satisfaction. Contentment. Fulfillment. A life so comfortable and worn and beautiful and vast and layered and yours completely that all the platitudes in the world couldn't contain it.

DAY 121

You don't need some elaborate morning routine. The whole point of any kind of wellness practice is to feel better, not to be stressed out trying to be better. This is your life. Pick a couple really key practices and add them into your day like sacred rituals. This is how you get to know yourself. This is how you center yourself. It's not about the perfect journal or the perfect water bottle or the perfect kitchen or the perfect anything. Write your thoughts on a napkin. Drink from a cup. Sit at your normal dining room table and connect back to what matters. Make it easy on yourself. The whole point of doing any of these habits is so you feel good. That is the point. It's for *your* benefit. Remember that. It truly does not matter how your life looks. It's always going to matter how it feels. And when it feels really good, who the hell cares how it looks?

DAY 122

You are stronger than your defense mechanisms, your distractions, and your avoidance tactics. You are strong enough to soberly face yourself and tell the truth to you, to admit what's working and what's not, and to crystallize a past regret into a future warning. You can be bold. You can take risks. You can be honest and you can be too much and you can be unruly and unacceptable and you can be judged by others—and you can still, above this, and above all else, like yourself and accept yourself and give yourself all the affirmation this world won't give you. You are strong enough to be defiant, to not conform, to not just do things because you think you should do them, to live to impress yourself. They don't tell anyone this enough: you are strong and you are bold and you are larger than your worst fears and you are better than your loudest insecurities. Who you were and who you've been is not who you are and who you will become. And, here's what they really don't tell anyone ever: you do not need anyone's permission to be whoever you want to be. All you need is *your* permission. And, the best part? You can give it to yourself right now.

DAY 123

I'm tired of striving. Of next levels and never settling and being in constant pursuit of bigger, better, more. I'm tired of "girlboss" and raising your standards constantly and always feeling like nothing is ever good enough. Sometimes I feel "wrong" for wanting a slower life, for accepting that imperfection will exist everywhere, including within *me*. Sometimes I feel "wrong" to want my growth to be a bit more steady and stable, to not always need to be pushing, but to let myself enjoy where I land before I'm already onto the next flight. I get tired of the constant and relentless dialogue to always be leveling up, pushing out of the comfort zone. "It's okay to want more" and it's okay to not, too. It's okay to have my life go in seasons, to follow up big changes and transformation with a settling in, not a "maximize and capitalize" plan. I don't want to feel like nothing is ever enough, that there's always some way I need to be improving and pushing and striving and hustling. I'm not a robot. I'm a human being and too often I forget that the being part is essential.

DAY 124

Change and healing is so hard. Staying the same, being in your comfort zone, doing things because everyone else does them, these are easy. Taking the path least traveled is lonely. There's a reason the beaten path is popular. This having hope thing and doing life authentically is not for the faint of heart. I'm sorry that it's taking longer than you expected. I'm sorry that it doesn't just happen overnight. Maybe it's not your moment to begin. Maybe it actually isn't the right time. Sometimes even with your best intentions, the timing isn't on your side. Maybe your resolve is being tested. Maybe it's your self-trust, knowing when you need to let go and when you need to hold on. Or, maybe it's the perfect time, and life is about to give you all the magic you've been waiting for. It's not easy listening to and trusting yourself over the status quo. It's not easy trying to better yourself and your life. I hope you take a moment today to acknowledge that and give yourself some love for getting up and trying again and again.

DAY 125

It's imperative, in your one life, to keep searching for whatever returns you to you. People give so much of themselves away. This world takes so much from them. You must relearn who you are. You have to undo what the culture tells you about what you should value in yourself and others. So, when you find someone, something, some creative work or some form of expression that returns you to you, a something that feels like coming home, it is critical that you pursue it, hold onto it, let it heal you. When you find something pure and genuine and real about yourself, something untainted, something that has persisted among the years of your life, it's imperative you honor that calling in some way. Find a way to feel useful and important. Find a way to feel that you matter. Give yourself that and if you haven't found it or you haven't found enough of it yet, keep looking and searching and digging deeper into yourself—and never stop finding those people, that art, the music, that friend, the lover, the anything that brings you back to you. You should always be looking for reasons that you matter. That you're special. And you should never discount your callings. Share them. Be bold. It's your one life. Reveal yourself.

DAY 126

Protect your peace for sure. But just remember that a lot of your best lessons are on the other side of instant gratification and on the outskirts of your comfort zone. Sometimes you have to work a bit at your peace before you have it to protect. A peace built on escapism and distraction is not real peace. A peace that demands you avoid conflict and never tell the truth, even to yourself, is not peace. A peace that has you denying what you really want to abstain from the risk of rejection and failure is not really peace. When your peace is built on you being your most fully expressed self, protect it. Don't settle for the *illusion* of peace that exists when you have to cramp and deny yourself for it.

DAY 127

It's a balance. Of passion and rest. Of productivity and flexibility. Of doing what needs to be done regardless of your current motivation and then taking heed of your feelings when they arise. It's a delicate dance between these contractions and contradictions. Sometimes you have to push yourself to keep going and sometimes you have to rein yourself in. Sometimes you have to acknowledge how you feel and act on it and sometimes your feelings are trying to tell you to stop out of fear. There is a wisdom in knowing yourself, your values, and what matters to you. Forget what matters to society. You opt into and out of whatever you need. Because what matters to you is the true gauge. Are you living in alignment with your soul? Do you know yourself? Are you aware of yourself? This is calm. This is what brings you unshakable peace within.

DAY 128

Your life may not unfold in the way you want it to. You may have to reimagine some dreams. You may have to be more tender or more gentle with yourself. You may realize that all your best laid plans may have been born from a need to prove to others how good you were at being good. Maybe some of your dreams were other people's dreams you assumed should be yours. Maybe you worked really hard only to find you didn't want what you thought you wanted. Maybe you want something simple. Maybe you want a grander life than you think you're capable of having. Maybe. Maybe. Maybe. It's never too late to want something new. It's never wasted energy if you've been able to know yourself deeper, to see the edges of your desire and joy just a bit clearer. Life isn't supposed to be a straight line. You can zig. You can chart off course. You can lose yourself and find yourself again. You can rise from disappointment. You can change your mind about everything you thought was certain. It's your life. Yours. In all your iterations of self, never forget how simple the truth is: your life. *Yours*.

DAY 129

When you have nothing left to prove, nobody left to impress, and all that matters is how you feel about your own life—that's when it begins. When you realize nobody else gets to determine the trajectory of your life—that's when it gets interesting. When you stop prioritizing other people's opinions of your life above your own—that's when you're free. And when you finally stop looking for the answers out there and look for the answers within—that's when you see who you are, what you actually want, and how you're going to spend the rest of your one wild, free life.

DAY 130

You know what takes courage? Deciding on following through. Opening up the calendar and staking claim to time in your schedule for what matters. Cutting through the distractions and clutter. Having a few priorities—and that's all. Setting boundaries around your time and energy. Believing in your will and desire more than your fear. Getting it done instead of getting it perfect. Stacking up the hours. Practicing without judging. Looking at fear and saying, "Ok, I hear you, but I'm going to do this any way." It's an optimistic force of will to believe in yourself. To bet on yourself. To love yourself enough to take what you dream about seriously. Trust that the act of *trying* will change you. Not how perfect you are at getting it right immediately. But, the trying. The doing. The failing. The going for it. The shaky steps you take forward will define your life.

DAY 131

Sometimes there is no silver lining. There is no finding strength. There is no seeing the bright side. Sometimes it's about acceptance. And that acceptance might feel jagged. It's not a clean line. Sometimes a choice will leave residues of regret, even when it's best for you. Sometimes you'll miss the people who you know you can't be around. I hope that when you are feeling sad and prickly and frustrated that there's a voice within you letting that be okay. It's not always a lesson. Sometimes you have to just sit with disappointment. Sometimes you need the heaviness to engulf you. Sometimes melancholy can't be "fixed." Sometimes there's nothing anyone can say that can take away your pain. And that's okay. You don't have to react perfectly. You don't have to plaster a smile on your face that feels like a grimace. Let yourself be where you are. Feel what you feel. So much of your pain comes from trying to control your life, your emotions, your reactions when it's not always possible to do so. Be where you are, no matter where you are. Let acceptance be the gift of this season. Jagged as it might be.

DAY 132

It's quite simple. Journal out your feelings so that you know yourself. Get outside as much as you can. Say kind things to yourself on a daily basis. Get off the screens and into your life. Eat mostly whole foods but don't be obsessive. Move your body in a way that you don't hate. Smile. Notice the good that is happening. Express gratitude for the beautiful things in your life. Hug your people. Tell them you love them. Ask for help. People want to help you. Remember that you are loved even when you don't think you are. Your life is lovely. Your life is lovely. Your life is lovely. Say it until you really, deeply believe it. You are alive. Today, you are alive. Don't underestimate how unbelievable that is. You get another day to notice how beautiful you and your life are.

DAY 133

Maybe through allowing it all—the good, the difficult, the uncomfortable—you end up more comfortable with it all. Isn't it funny how that works? That the uncomfortable can lead to the comfort. That the difficult can lead to the contentment. That the small details can lead to the big life. It goes against everything we've been told. But, you know, most great things in life often do.

DAY 134

Instead of treating life as if there's one perfect configuration that will make you happy forever, why not treat it like one big wonderful experiment? Take the pressure off completely. Give things a shot. Approach every new thing with a beginner's mind. Let life surprise you. Let an unexpected hobby become an all-consuming love affair. Let yourself be bad at some things, and enjoy the hell out of them any way. Let yourself improve, see the benefit of practice. Let yourself have a light grasp on all the things and achievements you think make up a beautiful life, and instead just dive in and try. Try anything. Try *everything*. And then trust what lights you up. Trust your joy. Trust what feels easy and what feels exciting to improve on. Trust where it flows. Trust what you love right when you wake up in the morning. Experiment until you find it. Then, keep experimenting. Because there's always so much more to discover, within yourself, and within this one endlessly interesting life of yours.

DAY 135

It's not about life being easy. There's so much out of your control. So much pain to witness and endure. To be alive is to have to deal with a hundred contradictions at once. The joy, the sadness, the injustice, the beauty. There will be suffering. It might get darker before it gets lighter. Healing isn't always pretty. Change isn't always welcomed. There is so much out there and within that is fighting against your desire to love and to see the good in others. All that is true and yet you can choose to let yourself be easy on yourself. You don't have to be your own worst enemy. You don't have to hoard your joy. You don't have to punish yourself. You don't have to be your own biggest barrier. Live lightly. Understand what is yours to carry and what isn't. See what you can change, where you can help, and focus there. Be a reason someone feels hopeful. Be your own reason to be hopeful. Let it all be a little lighter on your shoulders. Love is always more effective than despair. Remember that your empathy has to extend to you, too.

DAY 136

One day, with the benefit of retrospect, this will all make sense to you. Why you had to go on that detour. Why you were stuck in it for years. Why you had to generate self-belief. Why it felt like you were getting prepared. Why you had to heal before it all showed up. Why it hurt. Why your sadness overwhelmed you. All of it will mean something. All of it makes up the tapestry of your life. Trust that, even when it feels dark and uncertain, you are being led somewhere. Trust that you are being primed for magic, for synchronicities, for it all to one day come together so you can say: Oh, that's why. Trust you are being prepared. If you feel lost, that means you're going somewhere new. Not all of life can be perfect. You have to heal toward your bigger dreams. You have to become the person to contain more exciting opportunities. Trust it's all leading you there. Let go of the strict plans, but don't give up on the vision. It's all finding a way to work out for you.

DAY 137

How you measure your life is how you value your life. You may be tempted to measure it in the obvious, societal way. How much you earned and lost. The shape of your body. The amounts. The numbers. The metrics. And while those aren't necessarily unimportant, there are more interesting ways to measure. How much love you are able to give and receive and allow. How you've healed and live in the nuance of yourself. How you've grown, how many different versions of you you've let yourself become. How kind you are to yourself and to others. How compassionate. How's your heart? How's your hope? The measure of your life is too small when you put it into numbers. It's too limited. It doesn't encompass the complexity of you, of a life. How do you love? How do you respond in hard times? Who are you when nobody is watching? Can you be alone with yourself? Have you found a way to negotiate all the world's contradictions and still make time for joy? How alive are you to it all?

DAY 138

There's a surprising freedom in cultivating discipline. You're going to show up, regardless. You're going to get to it, regardless. You're going to believe in yourself, regardless. It's difficult to be hard on yourself about where you are in life when you're actively disciplining yourself to create a better future. Discipline is a generator, of confidence and self-respect and self-trust. It seems so militant on the surface. So restrictive. But in fact, ask any person who is disciplined, it's the opposite. It's a relief. A freedom. A joy. To be able to count on yourself. To lovingly line up who you say you are and what you actually do.

DAY 139

There's this fear that if you let go of control, everything will fall apart. But it's not true. What happens when you let go of control is that you release the tension of uncertainty. You stop forcing it all to happen and instead *let* it all happen. Releasing control can be scary at first, but then it's freeing. Because you are no longer under the illusion that you can control outcomes. You are living in a state of accepting exactly where you are and expecting that you will come into serendipitous alignment with whatever is most meant for you. Let life drive for a while. Let it be uncertain. Get lost and found again. Repeat that. Let yourself be taken with the flow of life and watch as it all lines up in the most surprising way that is better than all of your best laid plans.

DAY 140

Learn how to use your own definitions. What is your version of happiness? Of success? Of a life well-lived? Remember that nobody knows you better than you know yourself. Nobody has a map that'll lead you where you most want to go. Nobody can tell you when you're lit up by the joy of something. Nobody can know when you feel most you. Nobody can understand what joy and sadness and excitement and love feels like to *you*. Your life belongs to you. So, craft a definition of your most beautiful life. Find what makes you happy. Carve a you-shaped hole into this world. Let your own definition of success guide you. Stop waiting for permission to have the kind of life you most desire. Decide on what that life looks like and move yourself closer and closer to it each day. Take risks. Be bold. And start saying no to anything that doesn't fit within your definition. Your most beautiful life starts with you defining what that even looks and feels like for you.

DAY 141

There are many different routes to get to the same place. You can choose the hardest way. You can neglect yourself and your well-being to get "there" the fastest. You can force it all to happen, even when it doesn't feel right. You can stomp on others to get ahead of them. You can drive straight to your destination, frustrated, feeling "behind," and never once stopping to enjoy the view. Or, you can choose to go a little slower. You can relax, take the pressure off. You can work hard, commit, be consistent with small, sustainable steps. You can go with the flow of your life. You can love yourself through all the disappointments. You can get "there" and find you are still intact; your well-being came with you. You are still with you. You learned so much on the journey. You met a lot of interesting people. Some of those pit stops set the foundation for who you became. Some of those detours lit you right up. It might take a little longer this way, but hey, don't you think being in your life while you have it is worth slowing down for?

DAY 142

The peace you desire might cost you the life you think you
"should" have. You might need to choose your peace over
everything else. You might need to change your definition
of what a "good life" looks like. You might need to let go
and release some outdated ideas of success. You might need
to divorce what you want from what society wants from you.
You might need to pick a simpler life. You might need to save
your energy for what really matters to you. You might need
to sit in the stillness for a while and actually figure out what
really matters to you. You might need to ask yourself some
hard questions. You will need to be honest with yourself.
You will need to face yourself. You will need to heal. But
once you get a taste of that hard-earned peace, all the work
will be worth it. You'll never want to go back to who you
used to be ever again.

DAY 143

Nothing will build confidence and self-worth better than keeping your own promises to yourself. Taking action even when you don't feel "ready" yet. Letting the small steps stack up. Giving yourself the gift of progress. Not letting all of your what if's die within you or burn a hole inside of you from disuse. People think it's always the big moments, the big decisions, the rock bottom, the breakdown that leads to the change. But what you do every day—who you speak to, how you speak to yourself, how you show up, what promises you consider sacred, how you care for yourself—these are monumental shifts. Celebrate small progress. It all adds up. Your efforts are never wasted.

DAY 144

Healing is inner work, changes from the inside out, reckoning with the past. But please remember an important part of healing is the *integration*. It's doing things differently. Doing life differently. New words. New ways. New actions. Healing is internal and then to truly seal in your healing is to grieve and let go of the old self, let there be ample room for a new self to emerge. This is a vital part of the healing process. It's not just thinking new thoughts or analyzing over and over. It's showing up differently. Catalyzing a new self by embodying their rituals, habits, the way they move through the world. You cannot be a new self without this. Instead, you will end up circling the same drain of emotions, unclear why you're not moving forward. Embodying the new self, integrating the new information, learning how this healing has changed you and acting as if you are that new person— this will ground you. It will root you. You will shed an old skin and become someone you have never been before.

DAY 145

There are certain decisions that bring power to your life. A no that opens up the possibility for something much better. A yes that calls in a whole new experience. Some decisions feel like declarations. This is where I'm deciding to go. This is who I am now. This is what I deserve. A no can carry more than a yes sometimes. A no to what no longer fits, and isn't who you are anymore. A yes to what feels right, even if it's the strange choice that nobody else would make. Remember that when you're making decisions. Think about what new opportunities your no might carry in. What your yes is opening up space for. What your declarations are saying about the kind of life you are building. It's never random. All along, you are constructing and creating. A great no or a truly aligned yes can open up your path in the most powerful ways. Use them wisely.

DAY 146

The entirety of your life is filtered through your perception. Do you not see how you have to be careful what you think? Every perception you have is a perception of the mind. Every pain you have endured is given meaning in the mind. You have this incredible power to change your thinking at any point in time, yet you overestimate the need for external changes and underestimate perception shifts. The world is obsessed with the physical and tangible and not obsessed enough with how changing the mind changes the filter in which you view your entire life. People think they need more "things" in order to be happy. But the more people accumulate, the less they feel satisfied. There is nothing outside of you that will bring peace if you believe something outside of you is meant to bring you peace. Your purpose on this earth is not to follow trends until you die. You have no idea how significant your mind is, do you? How powerful and generative it is? How your entire life can change in just one perspective shift? Don't waste that miracle.

DAY 147

You think if you stop worrying, you'll stop being in control. You think your worry *is* control. You think if you prepare for every terrible scenario, it'll make it less devastating when they happen. You think that if you want a little less, maybe you will be spared the pain of failure. You think your anxiety is being productive, protecting you, warning you, creating a wall between you and your emotions, between you and life. Who would you be without this worry? Who would you be with hope? Who would you be if you surrender all your ideas of how it should be and let it be exactly what it is? Who would you be if you weren't pushing yourself? Who would you be if you trusted that what's next shows up perfectly? Who would you be if you realized this worry doesn't protect you from pain, but actually ensures you are always in pain? Who would you be if you stopped grasping those worries, let the ribbon go, and watched the balloon fly away? Would you be free?

DAY 148

Self-love doesn't feel like loving every single part of yourself at all times. No. Self-love is a *homecoming*. A safe space. A place to be exactly who you are. A soft spot to land in a hardened world. A listening within to how you really feel and a lack of judgment on the answer. It's your body and your mind at peace. It's a calm understanding that whatever happens, you've got your own back; you will show up for you. Self-love isn't something you can perfect and arrive at. It's an ongoing unfolding, unlearning, and becoming—all at once.

DAY 149

It can be the easiest thing in the world to constantly focus on the negative and the gaps where it's all not "working" yet. That's so easy. It takes concerted effort to see the little bread-crumbs that are saying you're on the right path. They are much more subtle than the bigness of anxiety and doubt. They feel insubstantial compared to panic and comparison. But they are nothing short of little miracles. And the more you focus on where it's all working, the more days you wake up and think: *wow, it's all working out for me*. It's not always a matter of external circumstance. In fact, it hardly ever is. It's a mindset. A state of perpetual faith.

DAY 150

It's important to remember that the pain of an event is caused by what you interpret that event to mean. The same thing can happen to someone else and they'd interpret it differently. What you make the situations in your life mean is what causes the pain. That doesn't mean you absolve others of responsibility or accountability, but that you take ownership over what stories you've created from what has happened. That sometimes you hold onto pain that can be let go, because you've created a story and identity around who you became because of it. The events in your life can be neutral. It's all about the emotions and stories you create from those events. And if you can be a gentle observer of those emotions, if you can stop a story from being created, then you can neutralize the event. It doesn't have to follow you or stay with you. It can be what it is—and it doesn't have to mean anything more than a thing that happened to a version of you in the past.

DAY 151

If you're asking for change, are you prepared to let go of the life you thought you should have? Are you prepared to let go of the stories that keep you in doubt and indecision? Are you prepared to get out of your head? Are you prepared to stop distracting and disassociating? Are you prepared to be audacious in your self-belief? Are you prepared to keep going when there is no evidence that you should? Are you prepared to surprise yourself? Be careful when you ask for change and "better." You may just get it, but first, you'll have to let go of everything standing in your way.

DAY 152

Every single time you take action when faced with doubt and resistance, you become more resilient. Every time you keep your promise to yourself when you don't "feel" like it, you become stronger. Every time you stare down the fear telling you it's not worth it, it'll never go anywhere, there's no point, and keep moving forward regardless, that fear becomes less intense. Every time you do not let yourself get discouraged, even when it seems like the evidence is stacked against you, an incredible resolve within you builds. Trust that your efforts are cumulative. It's one day at a time and the decisions you make when fear is trying to convince you to stay small, are the decisions that will define your entire life.

DAY 153

Maybe you don't need as much rest as you need more active engagement with your life. It's exhausting living out a checklist of societal norms. It's exhausting fulfilling everyone else's obligations. It's exhausting living a life that pleases others before it pleases yourself. It's exhausting waking up every day feeling disempowered. It's exhausting going through life when you're not number one on your own priority list. Or number two. Or ten. It's exhausting not living your truest self, out loud. It's exhausting ignoring the call of your soul for a little time spent on that one thing that keeps getting pushed off for "when things slow down." It's exhausting not honoring what you truly want. It's exhausting not taking any steps toward what you want. Maybe you don't need more rest. Maybe what you really need is a deeper connection to yourself, an existential reclamation that you matter, that you have agency, and that you are the one in charge of your own life. Because, when you're busy living authentically, it doesn't really feel that exhausting. It just feels like living out loud.

DAY 154

Most valuable tool you have within you? Your ability to be honest with yourself. You will be limited by your own dishonesty within. If you can't tell yourself the truth, or stand to hear your own truth, or be honest about your short-comings or mental blocks—you will stay a little small and cramped. Most people cannot be honest with themselves. They'd rather distract and avoid, become certain they know everything there is to know already. They can't stand to be alone with themselves. Being this way means you are likely going to live without really living. You can't trust someone who isn't honest which means you can't trust yourself. Being honest and aware of yourself is the best way to live authentically. And the greatest part? It's free.

DAY 155

There are a lot of opinions out there. A lot of information to consume. But I hope you know that at the end of the day the most important knowledge is within you. What feels true to you? What feels right to you? What lights you up? What excites you? What gets you up in the morning? Who are you when nobody is watching? *That's* the gold.

DAY 156

Truthfully, you need to admit that a lot of the things you think you need to make you happy are just ideas based on other people's lives. Your definition of success, unless you've really become conscious of it, is based on other people. Are you being honest with yourself? Until you are in concert with yourself, having a dialogue, and interrogating your belief system, it's entirely possible you are going through the motions, trying frantically to feel good in all the wrong places. You believe the gap between where you are and where you "should" be is a chasm. That's because you're trying to make your life look significant by other people's definitions. What if you... stopped? What if you stopped caring so much? What if you didn't have to do your life like anyone else? What would you want? What would you *really* want? This is available to you. This is your permission. Maybe instead of berating yourself for not being further along today, think about closing that gap altogether and stop caring about measuring up. It's freeing.

DAY 157

You can be healthy without being obsessive, each day choosing something a little more nutritious for yourself. Each day taking a walk or moving your body in some way. You can be emotionally well without avoiding your emotions. You can feel your feelings without them consuming you. You can find balanced ways to express yourself like journaling and talking to a friend. You can be productive with less time and less intensity. You don't have to crush it and go all in and let it take over your entire life. You can put in the hours consistently and build what you're building sustainably, instead of existing in high and low burnout cycles. You can have weeks or months that ask more of you and then weeks or months that you can slow it all down. It doesn't have to all be in balance every single day. *That's* a fulfilling life. It doesn't have to be so intense. You can work and spend time with people you love and eat well and express your emotions and at the end of a year, it adds up to something beautiful and balanced and lovely.

DAY 158

Have the courage to quit. Quitting something that is drain-
ing your energy is an expansive portal that is opening for
something new and better matched to come in. Quitting
and "no, not for me" are incredibly potent states of being.
Sometimes you have to let go and trust so that a new experience has space to come to fruition. Sometimes you cannot
get what is most aligned to you if you're still holding on
to something else out of fear. There are moments to build
resolve, and keep going. There is phenomenal insight in
committing and putting in the work. But there is also
something freeing and expansive when you quit. You have
space for something new. You have space to grow. You're no
longer contained. You are free to choose again. Having the
discernment and wisdom to know when it's time to commit
more or when it's time to quit is the key.

DAY 159

At any moment, you are free to make a perspective shift. Never undervalue the power of your mind to contextualize your life differently. You can legitimately change your mind about how you approach almost everything. You can work through an emotional limitation until it ceases to exist. You can process a past pain until the heat of it no longer burns you. It's astonishing, the way the mind can shift in your favor. Every experience is just your interpretation of it so if you change your interpretation, you fundamentally change the experience. It all starts within and at first, that realization might make your stomach sink. But then you realize just how much power you have within you to change your reality, your interpretation of your reality, and the actions you take based on what you believe internally. When you're lost, start within. It's the answer.

DAY 160

What if you trusted that it was all arranged for you? You're trying so hard to figure out how it will happen. You're working so hard, forcing it. You're hustling, thinking this is how you earn it. But, what if you followed your clearest intuitive voice? What if you trusted that if you keep showing up, it's all arranging for you? Maybe your plans are too small. Maybe you can't predict the way it's meant to unfold. Maybe you're blocking the magic by assuming you know what it's going to look like. Trust that it can be better than your plans. Apply this to anything you are questioning and worrying about in your life. *It's arranged.* Your life is not a destination to arrive at. It's an unfolding. And so, let it unfold. Let yourself be led to the next exciting thing. Let yourself release the grasp on trying to force it so that all the miracles, blessings, and lessons can find their way to you. Let go. Trust in doing so, you end up exactly where you're meant to be.

DAY 161

The only way to know your life is authentic to you is by living with intention. What that means is that you need to know yourself intimately. You need to add your wants and needs to your life from a blank slate. You may need to wipe it all clean before you can add anything back in. You need to choose how you want to feel about yourself and your life and you will need to vigilantly reframe your limiting beliefs. You'll need to figure out a way to connect to yourself on a daily basis. You'll need to stop listening to what they say is a "good life" out there and listen to your inner wisdom. You are not supposed to want all the same things as everyone else. You are not meant to live your life like a template. You are more than an accumulation of things that other people think are cool. Embrace where you are different. Embrace your rebellion of the status quo. Embrace your truest self, the still voice within that isn't trying to prove anything to anyone. That is your authentic self, the one that doesn't sound like anyone else. Your authenticity is not going to come from anyone out there. It's going to come from within and the only way to truly alchemize that person into being is by journeying inward. Your own personal odyssey of the self. Embark upon it. Become someone we've never seen before. Guide yourself back home to you.

DAY 162

It could all work out for you better than you could imagine. It could all slot into place when you least expect it. Your whole life can change in the span of an hour, a week, a month, a year. Stay open to the magic. Keep saying yes. When the good comes along, make sure you're ready to notice it.

DAY 163

Time and energy are *not* the same thing. You can have all the time in the world but if your energy is being drained by doubt, indecision, and anxiety, you are not going to feel that you have a surplus of hours in the day. If you spend more time overthinking and less time taking imperfect action, you'll feel exhausted by the end of the day. You need to experiment. You need to use your energy to create, instead of to destroy. You think you need more time, but most likely you need more self-belief. You need more action. You need an hour in the day where you aren't questioning yourself and, instead, just being consistent about taking your small steps forward. That hour per day can change your life. Never underestimate the power of a focused hour. The answer isn't to wait until you have more time. The answer is to shut the noise off, and do the next small step. Once you build up a series of steps, you'll notice how much more energized you'll feel. Momentum is a powerful thing.

DAY 164

Youth is not the only time for success and acclaim. You get better as you get older and it's about time we acknowledge that. That we normalize success at any age, because youth is too short to do everything you want to do in this one life. You can pivot. You can change. You can reinvent. You can surprise yourself. You never know when it's your time, your moment. The trick is to keep believing. To not give up on the things that matter the most to you. You are not past your prime. When you are feeling your best and doing things that light you up—*that* is your prime. Never let your chances go by because you're too fixated on age. The wisdom of age is a gift. Use it.

DAY 165

If you think your ultimate peace and happiness is only achievable through everything going right all the time, your life will be a perpetual problem to solve. If you think there are obstacles to your peace right this minute, you will always be on an obstacle course, trying to earn and perfect your way into happiness. If you do not believe that your peace can be developed from within, you will always look outside of yourself for it. You'll think the next achievement will finally make you feel good enough. You'll think that more and more will finally make you feel secure. You'll think this person has it better than you because they have accumulated more material of the world and stash it on a heap. When you know you don't need anything outside of you to bring you peace, the next step in your journey truly begins. It doesn't mean you don't want to achieve or improve. It simply means you don't stake your entire life's happiness on goals and modern achievement. When you know you can be peaceful anywhere, doing anything, that's nirvana.

DAY 166

Joy is more difficult and infinitely more valuable. Finding a way to feel good in a world that profits off people feeling bad about themselves is revolutionary. Be motivated by more joy, by feeling good, by affirming yourself even more. Seek media, people, experiences that make you feel good and worthy. The real work isn't in using shame to change, but in using love to change. The real work is in looking at all the ways you could feel inadequate and, instead, deciding to feel absolutely perfect the way you are. To look at your life and only see where you are thriving, not where you're lacking. To prioritize feeling really good, experiencing more joy, alleviating stress, and doing what's best for *you*.

DAY 167

The answer to envy isn't to avoid everyone and anything that makes you feel bad about yourself. It's about building up a strength of self. It's about building a trust within yourself. It's about listening more to what silently pulls you. Sometimes what pulls you isn't joy. It's discontent. It's discord with your true self. And envy is a strong discord. It's a lightning bolt into your current reality. And, if you take action on your envy, if you find a way to mold something uncomfortable into something useful and purposeful, you might just start building a life that hardly ever has space or time for jealousy.

DAY 168

The imperative in life is to stop trying to prove your worth to other people. To stop caring what other people think about you long enough to find out what *you* think about you. To discern between what you think you should do in order to keep up with others versus what you actually want to do. Once you've released yourself from external expectations, when your desires have nothing at all to do with how impressive they may seem to others, when you've done the hard work of loving yourself unconditionally—this is when goals become more exciting. You get to see what's left in the process of divorcing your worth from external praise. It's just you and you now, deciding how you'd like to spend your time on this earth. Do you want to work to afford all your hobbies? Do you want to leave a legacy of your work behind you? Are you really ambitious underneath it all? Who are you when you don't need praise from others? Who are you when you've affirmed yourself? What goals do you have now? They become a lot easier to discern and to work toward, once you've stopped putting your entire worth on achieving them. Now, goals are fun—seeing what you can mold from the clay of your life. They could all be the same desires as before, but now they're yours and nobody else's. Your life belongs to you. And *that* makes all the difference.

DAY 169

Consistency, habits, effort, hard work with your head down and nobody clapping for you—well, it might not be as sexy to everybody else as overnight success. That's true. There are a lot sexier ways to show up in this world. But, in terms of what will feel good to you when you tell it back to yourself—growth has everything beat. The process wins by a mile. Getting better at something through committed and consistent everyday steps is incredibly fulfilling. That's the good stuff right there. Because, sure, you don't get as much outward praise, but you get your *own* praise. And eventually, that counts for everything. Eventually, that becomes the only currency you want to spend.

DAY 170

Sometimes you're choosing discomfort when you need to choose peace. And sometimes you're choosing avoidance when you need to choose discomfort. You have this tendency to make the easy things harder than they need to be and the hard things easier than they need to be. It's a strange juxtaposition. There are certain things in your life that require you keep pushing past resistance and stepping into discomfort. When you are building a skill, mastering a craft, or intent on improving in a certain area. The discomfort, in that case, is proof of growth and progress. But you don't always have the capacity to do the harder things because you're often making the easier, simpler things a lot more complicated. You need to get outside, you need to eat more vegetables, drink more water, move your body, maybe add something mindful to your morning and call it a routine. Don't spend three hours of your day on a morning routine when you need to embrace the discomfort of learning a craft. Tending to yourself is *simple*. But actually giving space and time to what is calling to you—what will require your grit and determination—you ignore that and make everything else complicated. No. Do the opposite. That inner shift will change everything.

DAY 171

In order to truly change your life, you need to adopt more long-term thinking. But not in terms of more goals. Think in terms of your Future Self. They will arrive no matter what. What kind of life, right now, are you building for them? Are you giving them more burdens, shifting responsibility onto their shoulders? Or are you lightening their experience? Are you making life *easier* on them? For example, if you start going on a daily walk today, your Future Self a year from now is going to have increased fitness and mental clarity. If you start writing the book today, your Future Self might have a draft in hand to refine. What you put into practice today either helps or hinders your Future Self. You are becoming them whether you like it or not. But if you start today, your efforts become cumulative and your Future Self gets to reap the rewards. *This* is how you change your life. Thinking past instant gratification and, instead, into easing the burdens and making life more joyful for your Future Self.

DAY 172

You don't know what's coming around the corner. You don't know what's being prepared for you. You don't know what needs to miss you in order for something to find you. You just don't know. And you can spend your life thinking it's so stressful not knowing. Or you can spend your life thinking wow, this such an adventure. You have that choice. To relax into the unknown and trust the flow of your own life. Or you can resist it. Either way, life is going to do what it's going to do. You can either enjoy the ride or brace yourself for every moment of it. Up to you.

DAY 173

You're not behind on your own life. It's impossible. The big thing holding you back is the false belief that you're behind. You are comparing to other people if you think you're behind. You are following their timeline. You are thinking we're all supposed to have the exact same life, like there's some template you need to fit into. You don't know what lessons you still need to learn. You don't know what is lined up and arranged so that when your moment comes, you're ready for it in a whole different way. You don't know what you're here to do on this Earth, what path you're meant to walk. You think you know. There is no behind. There are no timelines for you. Get that thinking out of your head. Trust that you are exactly where you're meant to be. Seek evidence of that. And keep going. This is *your* path. Don't waver from it.

DAY 174

Your need for certainty will cost you an incredible life that will continuously surprise you. Your need for control will cost you the most amazing experiences you haven't even had yet. Your need for comfort will cost you the progress and mastery you crave so bad it aches. Don't become enamored with the false promises of certainty, control, and comfort. They will not save you. Pursuing them only guarantees you cut yourself off from all the life you haven't even lived yet. Life is made in the unknown leap. Without it, it's just one monotonous day into the next. Let life have your trust and see all the wonder left for you to discover.

DAY 175

How would you approach your life if you knew it was all working out for you? Even if you think you know exactly what will make you happy, life may have other plans for you. Can you let go of the control and grasping? Can you trust that when something has to be ripped from your life, it's meant to go, because maybe you weren't willing to unclasp your fingers from it? Can you hold to your plans lightly? Can you be open to your vision coming true in ways you would never expect? Can you be led, instead of forcing your own will to come into being? Can you respond to the flow of life, instead of trying to direct the flow in the direction you think you should be going in? If you can adopt the idea that life is trying to make it all work out for you in ways you could never imagine, you may be able to settle down long enough to let it unfold for you. If you're too busy and frantic, thinking you're behind on your own life, how can the insights get to you? The inspired actions? The downloads? Slow down for a moment. Let the next step find you in your peace.

DAY 176

Even when you make a decision you know is going to bring you more peace, it's okay if you also feel grief with it. You are leaving a version of you behind. You know better now. You have more wisdom now. But you are also grieving the life you thought you'd have. Whether it's a relationship, a career choice, anything. In making decisions, you cut off from other possibilities. It's okay to grieve what you lose on your way to peace. Even the best decisions come with loss, too.

DAY 177

Hope. It's about having hope in yourself. Hope that you'll hold yourself through the harder times, that you won't create stories about your worth based on how other people treat you. Hope that you will decide your own value. Hope that you will keep the fire of your dreams alive. Hope that you'll let your dreams shift and change, too. Hope that you won't hold yourself hostage to a past version of you. Hope that you'll be flexible in the way you evolve and grow. Hope that you won't turn off the tap of reinvention. Hope that you won't let societal expectations morph you into someone you don't recognize. Hope that you get to the truth of who you are and learn to operate from there. Hope that you can always renew yourself, reframe your thoughts, rewrite your narratives. Hope that you won't let this world burn out the light within you. Hope that you recognize the power of hope in a world that wants you hardened. Hope. Stay soft. Stay gentle. Stay right there with yourself through it all.

DAY 178

Self-care has become a buzzword now. Commercialized and adopted to justify any purchase or activity. Yet, real self-care, the kind that actually transforms you, is radical in a culture that demands relentless work and hustle. Self-care is power, claimed back to yourself. It's doing what you must to feel good, even if what you must do is difficult and uncomfortable. It's taking care of your future self more than cashing in on instant gratification. It's knowing who you are in a system that tries to turn you into someone you're not. It's journaling your rage. It's finally going somewhere new. It's small and significant actions that prove to yourself you are worth your own care. It's proving to yourself your own value. Self-care is not a commercialized product, an eye-roll-inducing-trend. It's reclamation. It's *power*. It's you not outsourcing your well-being. It's you resisting the system. Every nap when you "shouldn't" is a middle finger to burnout. Every minute spent doing what is best for you instead of what is expected of you is a tiny revolution. Every time you choose yourself you are claiming yourself. Self-care is power in action.

DAY 179

Life will break your heart. People will break your heart. What's the answer? You close yourself off from life so nobody and nothing can hurt you? If you close yourself off, you miss *everything*. You miss everything worth living for. Let life break your heart. It is proof you are alive, that you are human, that you are existing with it all. The highs, the lows, and the ordinary between. Every single part belongs. Without the risk, there is no potential for heartbreak. But without the risk, there is no potential for that indescribable feeling that you are alive—truly alive—to your own life. You know the feeling. When you feel as though you are fully present to what's happening, your heart is swooping, life is responding, and all you have to do is breathe. You miss every bit of what it means to be alive when you close your heart. You miss it all. It's not worth it. By shielding yourself from getting hurt, you are in pain all the time. So, let life break your heart. It's proof you are truly living.

DAY 180

It's time. You're ready. You have to start living. Get out there. Make mistakes. Take risks. Do the unrealistic thing. Go out into the world and let your heart guide you. At some point, you need to take all this self-growth you've been doing and put it to use out there, out in your life. You'll have to get disappointed and rejected and heartbroken and then you'll get excited and chosen and watch as your heart mends itself. No matter what you achieve or how much inner work you do, you can't escape living and how it'll surprise you and ask for your trust and twist your plans and bring you somewhere you could never imagine for yourself. At some point, you'll have to release the reins of control and let life do what it does best: lead you not to what you think you want most, but what you need most. So, go. Take that risk. Do that thing you have no idea is going to work out and just try. Experiment. Put yourself out there. Get out of your comfort zone. Let life take the wheel. Let go and trust that maybe where you're going is better than all your best laid plans.

ABOUT THE AUTHOR

Jamie Varon is a writer, novelist, and creative entrepreneur.
She is dedicated to helping other people recognize the truth
within themselves, instead of outsourcing it to others. Along
with authoring *Radically Content, Radically Content: The
Journal, Main Character Energy: A Novel*, she has created
a unique digital course called Live with Intention which is
a highly-practical methodology on building self-trust. She's
also a sought-after creative consultant and graphic designer.
She describes herself as multi-passionate.

JAMIE VARON

ACKNOWLEGDMENTS

To anyone who has connected with my writing, thank you. For two decades, I felt like an outsider who was deeply misunderstood. Through sharing my writing, I have gained not only confidence, but the knowledge that I am not alone.

Made in the USA
Middletown, DE
11 September 2024